THE MENTORSHIP EDGE

THE
MENTORSHIP
EDGE

Creating Maximum Impact through Lateral and Hierarchical Mentoring

THE MENTORSHIP EDGE

DEBORAH HEISER, PhD

WILEY

Published by John Wiley & Sons, Inc., Hoboken, New Jersey.
Published simultaneously in Canada.

For general information on our other products and services or for technical support, please contact our Customer Care Department within the United States at (800) 762-2974, outside the United States at (317) 572-3993 or fax (317) 572-4002.

Wiley also publishes its books in a variety of electronic formats. Some content that appears in print may not be available in electronic formats. For more information about Wiley products, visit our web site at www.wiley.com.

Library of Congress Cataloging-in-Publication Data

Names: Heiser, Debbie, author. | John Wiley & Sons, publisher.
Title: The mentorship edge : creating maximum Impact through lateral and
    hierarchical mentoring / Deborah Heiser.
Description: Hoboken, New Jersey : Wiley, [2025] | Includes index.
Identifiers: LCCN 2024025263 (print) | LCCN 2024025264 (ebook) | ISBN
    9781394267118 (cloth) | ISBN 9781394267132 (adobe pdf) | ISBN
    9781394267125 (epub)
Subjects: LCSH: Mentoring. | Interpersonal relations.
Classification: LCC BF637.M45 H45 2025 (print) | LCC BF637.M45 (ebook) |
    DDC 158.3—dc23/eng/20240708
LC record available at https://lccn.loc.gov/2024025263
LC ebook record available at https://lccn.loc.gov/2024025264

Cover Design: Wiley
Cover Image: © berCheck /Adobe Stock
Author Photo: © Deborah Heiser

SKY10085538_091924

To my favorite people in the whole world. I love you!
Joel Weinberger
Liam Weinberger
Aiden Weinberger
For my dad, Larry Heiser

Contents

Introduction   **ix**

1 We Are Built to Mentor   1

2 Five Key Components to Mentoring   17

3 What Mentoring Isn't   27

4 Why We Mentor   45

5 Mentoring Styles   67

6 Mentors in Our Lives   87

7 Mentoring in the Workplace   109

8 Defining Mentoring through Research   141

9 The Future of Mentoring   157

10 Creating Culture through Mentorship   165

11 Call to Action: Finding Mentorship Opportunities   179

References   **189**

Acknowledgments   **193**

About the Author   **195**

Index   **197**

Introduction

I dread cocktail parties. Someone introduces themselves, we exchange pleasantries, and then they ask what I do. My reply, "I'm an aging specialist," stops them in their tracks. Their eyes glaze over. Their jaws slacken, and it's clear that drool is only seconds away. Then, their eyes dart around the room as they look to make a great escape from the most boring person in the world.

It wasn't always this way. In my late teens, I'd fly down to Florida to visit my grandparents during winter breaks. The flights from New York were easy and inexpensive, so I went often. My grandma was a ton of fun with a closet full of fabulous clothes, just my size. Even though she had emphysema, which worsened each year, she was always excited to see me, thrilled to take me to an early bird special dinner, to show off her grandkid to her friends, and we played endless games of canasta. Over the years, she remained as fun as ever but would need to go to the hospital more often.

On one visit, Grandma wasn't happy. In fact, she was cranky, snappish, and unkempt. No one could get her out of her funk. She didn't want to play canasta, read books, or go anywhere. Her usual fashionable outfits were downright grungy, and her hairstyle resembled the Heat Miser from the Christmas TV cartoons. No family member could determine why Grandma changed from bubbly and well groomed to crotchety and scruffy. One afternoon, my family met the psychologist who worked at the independent living center where she lived. We asked whether there was anything they could do for her. The psychologist said, "Your grandma is depressed. And, yes, I can help her." And she did. Grandma got back to herself in a few months. In fact, she was better than ever! Her hair was done, she was dressed to the nines, and lo and behold, Grandma landed a boyfriend—Wilbur. She went from zero to hero in months, and I was hooked on the power of psychology and the focus on aging. I moved from wanting to work in business to wanting to fix grandmas—to help them with depression and whatever else plagued them. I changed my college major from business administration to psychology to help cure grandmas.

When I graduated college, I started work at a psychiatric hospital in Westchester County, New York, as a research assistant with a consortium of aging researchers studying depression. How perfect! I dove headfirst into this opportunity and found it very rewarding. Consequently, I decided to pursue a doctorate in psychology. This was the 1990s, and when I looked for graduate programs, I found it incredibly difficult to find programs that offered a specialty in aging as part of a clinical or developmental psychology doctoral degree. The field of aging at the time was like the Wild West. This frontier was wide open and barely inhabited by research or interest. I chose Fordham University for two reasons: I wanted to stay in New York and a professor there had a mild, peripheral interest in aging. Although aging wasn't his primary focus, he was amenable to mentoring me. I joined the local, state, and international organizations for aging. I became active in every way possible with the excitement of a pioneer looking for gold on the West Coast. It was an inspiring time, but there still weren't many people studying aging, and most of those who did focused on Alzheimer's disease, depression, frailty, and everything else we all want to avoid.

Aging was a dread that loomed in the back of everyone's mind—that thing that people feared and no one talked about. Telling people I worked in the field of aging was like telling them I had leprosy. Cocktail parties . . . well, you already know what a roaring success those were. Nonetheless, I was moving full steam ahead, publishing, presenting, getting grants, and fully active in local and international aging organizations. I was feeling pretty confident about the mark I was making in the field of aging. It was surprising that I'd progressed so far in this area of research I'd never even given a second thought to a short time ago.

I felt my oats with my newfound success in a new field, full of hope and exhilaration. I was invited to a dinner at an upcoming conference. Imagining myself telling the dinner participants all about my achievements was fueling the days leading up to the event. A multitude of people I admired would be there, and the thought of listing off all of my work accomplishments had me giddy with excitement. The evening of the dinner party, I couldn't wait for my turn to talk because this was a group of researchers. Researchers love to hear about other people's research, so I was sure I would be the belle of the ball. As each person took their turn around the table talking about their work, the hum of my thoughts whirred, and I didn't hear a thing they said. When my turn came, I unleashed myself and my work upon them, going on and on about depression, frailty, and dementia.

As I waited for the excited responses from everyone, I looked around, and no one looked at all interested. A few seconds passed (a million awkward minutes), and someone across from me asked, "Why do you study aging?" I thought this was a strange question. How could it not be obvious? Didn't he understand the importance of mitigating the distress of older adults? My reply rolled right off my tongue. "Well, I'm trying to help alleviate suffering and frailty and help make palliative care accessible for optimal end-of-life care." I thought, "Duh." Then he said, "So you are telling us we have nothing to look forward to. Our future is bleak. All you are doing is putting a Band-Aid on our eventual pain, suffering, and death."

His words felt as if I had driven into a brick wall at 100 mph. I was stumped. I didn't have an answer, and I was embarrassed because I felt good about myself and the work I'd been doing. For God's sake, I won an international award for depression research, was getting grants, publishing, and speaking. I was active in organizations to promote aging. I was killing it. Or so I thought.

That dinner was an aha moment for me. I said to myself, "He's right!" Why was I bothering with all this if I was simply putting Band-Aids on our future? What does anyone have to look forward to? I suddenly became fearful. What if life was just an inverted V shape, and I was nearly at my peak. Panic set in as I slunk back to work a few days later. My strategy was to hit the books, journals, and theoretical work in developmental psychology to figure out whether I should bother continuing to study aging. I hoped I'd find anything we could look forward to as we grow older.

For years, I'd worked with older adults in psychiatric hospitals, nursing homes, and home health care. Pathology was the norm in what I was researching and seeing daily. I had to wrench myself away from that focus and return to my developmental psychology roots, which look at norms and what we should look forward to in life rather than pathology. The field was a treasure trove of hope and positivity that wasn't talked about in the popular research at the time: Alzheimer's, depression, and frailty. This wasn't what I wanted to look forward to. No wonder everyone ran away from me at cocktail parties!

I got excited by the work of Erik Erikson, whose theory of adult development had been around for decades and was ground-breaking but not a mainstream focus in aging. Erikson's theory posits stages in our lives that go beyond puberty, where most development theories end. The middle and older adult stages fascinated me. They offered emotional treasures that can befall all of us: meaning, value, and fulfillment. These emotional aspects of aging are almost never discussed. The emotional growth that occurs even while our physical decline is taking place. I spoke with Dr. Dan McAdams, a psychologist and professor at Northwestern University, who is essentially the demigod of Erikson's stage of generativity, a point in our lives we reach in midlife where we want to give back without expecting anything in return. After talking with Dan, I pivoted from focusing on the negative aspects of aging to the positives we can look forward to as we grow older.

I dove headfirst into studying how we develop past puberty. Our physical trajectory looks like a mountain—a steep incline beginning at birth, peaking in our 20s, followed by a steady decline for the remainder of our lives. It is essentially an inverted U. But what I'd never noticed and was keen to focus on was the emotional trajectory we all have. And it takes place at the same time as our physical trajectory. It is a slow, steady incline that never declines as we age. It is a straight line. This explains why most people become happier as they grow older, not depressed. Even when they can't run as fast or need glasses for reading. Midlifers don't generally care that they can't run as fast as they could when they were 20. But they like having close relationships with friends and family, as well as skills and expertise they've amassed over time. Finding this was striking gold. I felt that we'd been wasting our most precious natural resources. Us! We cast ourselves away as worthless as our value increases. I wanted to share this newfound treasure with everyone.

Midlife and generativity are the life stages I really glommed onto. This is when we emotionally come into our own with expertise, values, skills, and knowledge. Generativity encompasses three areas: mentorship, volunteering, and philanthropy, and it offers us a way to put back into the world what we've honed over time in a way that has our stamp on it. It is a legacy and a way to make our mark on the world. I decided that I needed to look at one aspect of generativity rather than all three because that would be overwhelming. I thought, "Well, okay, two of those are free. You can be anybody and volunteer or mentor. Not everyone can donate funds." So I took philanthropy off the list. Then, volunteering is something many of us desire to do, but it generally involves tagging onto someone else's passion or idea. Whether volunteering in a soup kitchen or a docent at a zoo, volunteering may not have everyone's personal passion attached to it.

Mentoring, on the other hand, is tailored to the mentor. It is a way to give back what we've been spending decades amassing: our expertise, skills, and values. Whether we are passing on leadership skills or how to make the best chicken soup, it is a way we can leave our footprint and have a lasting legacy. Volunteering comes close, but we work on someone else's dream or initiative when volunteering. Mentoring is a way to pass a piece of ourselves on, making us immortal. This is how religion has been passed down for centuries. This is how we've made enormous progress in technology and why we don't have to keep reinventing it. We can build on what we already know and grow from that.

I was so deeply fascinated by what mentoring offers us that I interviewed about 40 people in midlife, from a four-star general to a stay-at-home grandma, to see how and why they mentor. As it turns out, they all mentor the same way. They all have a purpose in mind. They all have their values in mind. They all have meaningful connections in mind. And these core principles really motivate them because the desire to give back is an intrinsic motivation. No one gets paid to do it. Like reading a bestselling book or putting together a puzzle, we do it because we want to. Everyone is engaged in mentoring in the same way, even though they all had very different life experiences.

The fantastic thing is that mentoring doesn't end with the emotional upswing we get when passing information and skills to others. The meaningful connections we cultivate in mentorship make mentors live *longer, healthier, happier lives*. It's not just something we do because we want to leave a legacy; it helps us live better and happier.

During my conversations with mentors, I spoke with Jim Moriarty, who saw a lot of combat in the Vietnam War. When he returned, he went to college and then to law school. Jim invented the mass tort law and became hugely successful. He is a legend in the law profession. He was telling me about the cases he fought and won. He was a knight in shining armor for many, responsible for enormous positive change for thousands of individuals. He was a guy on top of the world, and his story was surprising. Jim reminds me of a crusading Harvey Specter from *Suits*, but with a kind heart and Southern charm. He took on the impossible, and everyone knew he could and would win. He told me how a woman approached him and said, "Hey Jim, you're the only person I know who can help me. I have renal failure, and my workplace is not willing to pay for my kidney transplant. And I need one, or I'll die." She didn't have long to live. She needed a kidney transplant because she had a medical issue, not because she engaged in a lifestyle that might be correlated with renal failure. Jim was quite sympathetic and knew he needed to help her, but he also knew acting as her lawyer wasn't right. He told her, "It sounds like you're nearing the end of life. I can fight and win this battle, But you'll be dead by the time it's won. And I can guarantee you I'll win it, but you won't be able to even recognize that you've won."

He said something that sparked an aha moment for her. He said, "Go out, raise the funds, get yourself the kidney you need, and move forward. Just do that because then you'll have your life." Jim could have taken her money, and he could have fought the case. It would have been another win. But he decided to counsel her on how she could get through this life stage and regain her life. He gave her something to look forward to and mentored her through how she could take control of her life and win it for herself. They continued their conversation, and one day, she returned to him and said, "Hey Jim, I got my kidney. And I also got a kidney for about 1000 other people." The spark Jim put in her and the guidance he gave to get her started turned into a full-blown flame. She started a nonprofit to get kidneys for others. She got one for herself but didn't stop there; she continued making changes for many others.

Jim could see that he mentored her about something that saved her life: focusing on winning an argument with others vs. winning your life. Focus on you. Jim's mentee lived a full life, and other people did as well because when he passed the baton to her, she carried it and kept moving it forward. Countless lives have been saved because of this, and he says mentoring is the most meaningful thing a person can ever do.

All of his work and armed forces success can't compare to the fulfillment he feels when mentoring others. Jim still thinks about her and cries when he recounts it. Jim's story made me realize that there's something really, really powerful about mentoring. After we spoke, I said, "Hey Jim, do you know anybody else who mentors?" He said, "Yeah, you have to talk to my colleague's husband. He mentors kids on the weekends."

I knew I needed to speak with him. Mentoring was something that got Jim going. I needed to know whether mentoring mattered to others, too. When I spoke with this new contact, he didn't talk about innovation or , which he was known for. He was jazzed by his interpersonal interactions with his engineering mentees, one of his areas of expertise. He took pride in launching these kids into the world and helping them create their patents. I found that to be fascinating because it was nothing he ever publicized. His motivation was intrinsic.

I learned from these two people that mentorship followed Erikson's theory of generativity. But it differed from how it was discussed in the workplace, schools, and personal lives. I kept hearing about mentorship as something that the mentee has to go and find. There is always an elusive mentor, and we are expected to see who will help us. We never hear about the mentor. They are a faceless, nameless individual. There wasn't any thought about a mutual relationship. Instead, mentorship was described as a "grab the baton of knowledge and run through the open door" endeavor. But these two men put a face and a name to mentorship and described it as deeply meaningful and life-changing for them. Another aha moment for me. This was the first time I'd considered mentorship from the mentor's perspective.

After these two conversations, the engineer said, "Why don't you talk to my friend 'Ches'?" It turns out Bill "Ches" Cheswick is the guy who is one of the fathers of the network firewall. He's a former Bell Labs guy, and I figured this would be a great conversation. After all, he must be swamped with mentees because he's well known and well regarded. But instead, Bill said to me, "You have no idea how hard it is for me. I'm retiring and don't have anyone to share my information with; it's really bothering me. I am sitting here, full of energy and the ability to give back, and I can't find anyone to give back to."

I was shocked. Bill said, "I want to go to the fourth grade and younger little kids before they're jaded about math and science. I want to teach them STEM before they think they can't do it, before they think their paths are set. I want to teach quantum mechanics to fourth graders." Shocked but unsure how to help him, I said, "Okay, let's see what comes up." I never thought anything would come up. After all, who doesn't want to be mentored by someone of his caliber? But to my surprise, his situation was the norm.

I found and spoke with many people who didn't have access to mentees. And the higher their level, the fewer mentees they had. They simply didn't have access to mentees, and mentees had no way of finding them. I'd heard all the talk about "go find a mentor," but I'd never heard anyone say, "Go find a mentee." It was another one-sided story, and people needed to be connected. This conversation was when I fully realized that our world was in danger. We've been wasting our most precious natural resources—our knowledgeable, skilled experts because they can't find mentees. It made sense after speaking to several people like Bill, who were retiring. Their world was work. They didn't hang around kids or those just entering the workforce. It wasn't like they could go to a park and say, "Hey kid, wanna learn quantum mechanics?" People were reinventing the wheel repeatedly because they didn't have someone to pass the torch of knowledge to them.

Getting back to Bill. Nothing came up as I continued interviewing people about mentoring, with no particular goal in mind. But that changed about a year later. Someone said, "Hey, I think I can get us into schools." So I called Bill, and he said he was still interested; the engineer was too. I called my dad (an artist and web developer), Irene Yachbes, a former NASA engineer, Gabriel Lews, a college student, and Jura Zibas, an IP attorney my husband knew. Everyone wanted in. And we needed every one of these amazing mentors. Each wanted to mentor and saw this not as a bottomless pit of work without pay but as an opportunity to give back to students. We became the original founders of The Mentor Project.

Jura helped me get the incorporation documents in order, my dad, Larry Heiser, created the website, and Irene got mentors set with Girl Scouts and mentored in classrooms on Long Island. Gabriel Lewis, a college student, joined and got Bill into schools in New Jersey, and the engineer, Bob Cousins mentored students via Zoom. Everyone was having a ton of fun. We talked about expanding, getting into more schools, and doing all this with $547 in the bank account we set up. Realizing that this organization was being powered by highly accomplished, motivated individuals meant money wasn't needed to fuel the work. Everyone pitched in. My dad was making penny battery kits for the Girl Scouts, Bill was meeting with homeschoolers each week, which was set up by Gabriel, Bob was on Zoom with students, Irene and our growing group were meeting with Girl Scouts in classrooms on Long Island and the Bronx, and Jura was making sure we were filing everything and running as we should. We happily mentored all over the tri-state area, with Bob on Zoom on the West Coast. Then Jennifer Snow joined. It was 2019, and she was a Lt. Col and chief technology officer and intelligence operator with the Air Force.

Jennifer wanted to help us scale. It was exciting to expand with a few more mentors and start thinking about projects for students to work on in groups. Then the unthinkable happened. A mere six months later, COVID hit. We thought we were done. Schools were closed, and the world shut down. But that was really just the beginning for us. One door closes and another opens. People came out of the woodwork and asked to join The Mentor Project as mentors. Mathematicians, an astronaut, astrophysicists, a puppeteer, and several more. Then, Jennifer reached out to the contacts she was working with on a global free-access ventilator project. By May 2020, we had 60 mentors. In six months, we grew to six times our original size. We were still operating with less than 600 dollars in the bank, but mentoring moved to Zoom. We were mentoring in Argentina and across the United States, hosting international hackathons and a mask-a-thon, and our mentors were giving talks on Zoom to students worldwide. We suffered Zoom bombings in the beginning, time zone issues, and Internet bandwidth problems, but nothing stopped us. We reached thousands of students worldwide, and our mentor database kept growing.

Our mentors weren't just mentoring students (all virtually at this point). They also started mentoring each other. It was like an anthropological expedition. Mentors met regularly online to meet and learn from each other. These became weekly mentor meetups on Fridays. Mentors would hop on Zoom for an hour and give updates, formal presentations, and chat. It turned out our mentors weren't just enjoying each other's company. It was as if they'd been dropped into a candy store. They were mentoring each other, something I coined lateral mentoring™. They started working on projects together. Coauthoring articles, workshops, and books. In one case, a chief learning officer and a professor of linguistics, paired up to write an article for *Nature* based on a conversation in one of the meetings. Mentors connected at deeper levels than expected, celebrating birthdays, milestones, and book launches and helping when times were tough. One mentor drove another home from a colonoscopy, and another offered her apartment for someone to stay in while in town for a medical procedure. Mentors started meeting outdoors for group picnics and rooftop parties. It started to become a family of people who had a burning desire to give back and finally met others who had the same urge to pass on their knowledge, skills, and values. They didn't expect the hunger to learn from experts in completely different areas from their own. They began lateral mentoring™ (mentor to mentor) and still meet weekly to present, discuss, and catch up. We became a community of mentors.

Harnessing the Power of Mentorship

The power of mentoring goes well beyond a one-to-one relationship. It is more than a one-way street and much more than just hierarchical. Mentoring is something we are built to do and have been doing since the beginning of time. We've passed down religion for centuries, keeping faith and values relevant today. Our Founding Fathers came together with a range of expertise to create the United States. The tech revolution was built on mentorship. And, now, with our growing aging population, we are at the peak of possibility with mentorship. We can harness the good we all have in us to pass on to the next generation and those on our left and our right. Mentorship is a web of meaningful connections supporting, guiding, and propelling us forward.

Everyone said getting high-level experts to commit to mentoring was impossible. We thought we were a group of weirdo eccentrics just having fun. We are now more than 100 mentors strong with a wait list of eager mentors waiting to onboard. From comedy writer to science writer, astronaut to artist, entrepreneur to engineer, chemist to psychologist, our mentors are a bridge to the future. We carefully vet our mentors, and no one gets paid. We are fueled by donations, intrinsic motivation, and the knowledge that we are all crafting our legacies. To date, hundreds of hours of online content, podcasts, several patents, research, hackathons, innovation lab meetings, and an annual trip to Tanzania to teach art are just a few of the accomplishments our band of mentors has put into the world. The idea is to give back for free to ensure any student anywhere in the world can receive mentorship. Artist Justin Thompson traveled halfway around the globe to Shirati, Tanzania, to teach them cartooning. Fifteen students were selected to receive the Larry Heiser Art Scholarship. They received online art lessons each month with Justin (who got up at 4 a.m. to teach the class on Zoom each month).

One thing we've learned, beyond the theory that we're built to give, is that we are connected people, and whether we mentor in the workplace or in a rural area of Tanzania, we mentor in exactly the same way. Mentoring is the same whether we are mentoring corporate leadership, entrepreneurship, astrophysics, or puppetry. Mentoring isn't a unique, secret activity available only to the fortunate. Mentors aren't experts based on their education. They aren't in the "up" position. Mentees and mentors are both equal participants in the equation. And now that we have a modern form of mentorship with AI and online capabilities, mentorship can expand more rapidly than ever before. It is ready to explode.

This book is more than a chronicle of my journey; it's an exploration of the inherent human capacity for mentorship. It delves into the theory, practices, and diverse manifestations of mentorship across various disciplines. Drawing on the experiences of mentors from comedy writers to astronauts, it unveils the transformative potential of mentorship—a universal endeavor that knows no bounds.

As you embark on this exploration, you'll discover why we are inherently built to mentor, what defines good mentorship, and how it can be applied in diverse settings. Whether you're aspiring to be a mentor or seeking guidance as a mentee, this book is your map in the rich landscape of mentorship.

The Mentor Project is not just a narrative; it's a call to action. It's an invitation to become part of a community dedicated to passing on the torch of knowledge, skills, and values. Join me on this journey, and let's unlock the immense potential of mentorship that lies within us all.

1

We Are Built to Mentor

At birth we begin an emotional journey that propels us from the vulnerability of infancy, where we rely on trust in those who care for us, to the autonomy of childhood, where we eagerly embrace new experiences and master skills. This climb continues from adolescence, where we form our enduring identity, through young adulthood, where we form meaningful relationships, through later adulthood, where we focus on productively giving, and culminating in our senior years, where we reflect on our life's journey (hopefully positively).

Our early years largely focus on our physical development. As we get older, we must shift from the physical trajectory, which has a steep incline from birth through our early 20s, where our physical abilities peak, and then a steady decline (Figure 1.1). Most of us focus on our physical trajectory, which makes growing older scary. What most don't recognize is that our emotional course follows a steady incline from birth until our last breath (Figure 1.2). Our emotional path never declines! As we age, our emotions serve as guiding forces, prompting us to continue to evolve, to share our accumulated wisdom, and to shape a legacy that fulfills us. We are happier as we grow older despite our physical trajectory. I am 55 as I write this, and as I say to my undergraduate students

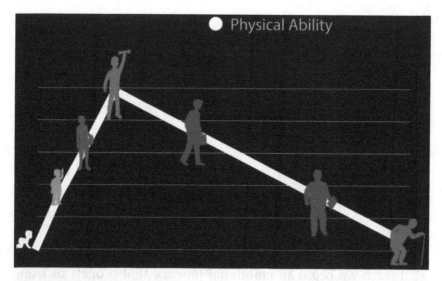

FIGURE 1.1 Physical activity.

FIGURE 1.2 Emotional growth.

each semester, "I can't run as fast as you, but I am happier than I was when I was your age." This is typical for adults. As we need reading glasses, can't run as fast, and gather wrinkles, most of us wouldn't trade our emotional well-being for that when we were 18, wrinkle- and reading glasses-free. I worked with a client who was in his mid-70s, suffered from COPD, and had very limited mobility. I asked how he felt. He said, "I feel just fine. I can read, work on the computer, and see my children and grandchildren." Others assumed his physical state would deem him miserable, but he was just the opposite. He was satisfied with his life. He wanted to live longer and looked forward to each day.

Our emotions inspire continuous self-improvement, a desire to share our knowledge with others, and the creation of a legacy that resonates with purpose. The stages these emotions help to create are universal. They transcend geographical boundaries, financial status, and work. **We are inherently wired to share rather than hoard our emotional wealth.**

Consider the iconic cartoon character Daffy Duck, comically standing atop a mound of riches, exclaiming, "Mine, mine, all mine." The humor lies in recognizing that wealth alone does not define our core desires. Reflect on the actions you take for yourself and compare them to those you perform for others. Most people don't want to stand alone with a pile of riches but would rather share them in joy with others. As we navigate through life, we rarely consider the emotional dimensions that underlie our choices, overlooking the importance or value of our emotional life. We don't think about how good it feels to share, to see the world through the eyes of someone as they unwrap a gift we know they'll treasure. Think of any Hallmark movie, with the grandparent taking the grandchild fishing and the joy that is the classic calling card that makes those movies popular.

In film, cinematic narratives vividly portray characters who undergo transformative journeys, mirroring the dynamics of real-life emotional growth. Take, for instance, the Grinch, whose self-serving nature initially compels him to sabotage the joyous celebrations of others. However, his heart undergoes a profound transformation when he discovers that true fulfillment comes from giving and fostering meaningful connections. The adage "'Tis better to give than to receive" is psychologically and empirically true. The examples in film are accurate in life too. We get so much from giving. It feels as if our own hearts grow three sizes when we see others accepting our gifts, whether they be a coveted physical gift or an abstract transfer of knowledge or wisdom.

Fictional characters such as Ebenezer Scrooge exemplify the innate human desire to give back, transcending material wealth in search of genuine joy. I call this the Ebenezer effect. Scrooge was a self-made man, wealthy, living in a mansion with servants taking care of his every need. But he was miserable until he became generative (having an innate urge to care for others without expecting anything in return) and gave back. As soon as he shared, he felt joy. The story works because this is how it is in real life, too. Although outliers may exist—individuals who cling to their riches without sharing, focusing solely on themselves—such instances are exceptions rather than the norm, and many/most individuals undergo transformative changes before the end of their lives.

We, as individuals, become mentors not merely out of duty or a sense of responsibility but to experience the profound sense of being needed, useful, valued, and purposeful. We experience the joy of seeing our torch of wisdom being accepted by our mentee. Mentoring is a reciprocal exchange, providing validation, relevance, a lasting legacy, and a sense of profound meaning. As our physical bodies inevitably undergo negative changes with time, our minds and emotions continue to expand, fostering a journey of generativity that enhances the quality of our lives. Feeling validated, useful, valued, purposeful, and relevant are all basic emotional needs we are built to seek, and they bring us fulfillment because we understand (even if not consciously) that mentoring provides us with a legacy, meaning, and fulfillment. We aren't just checking boxes leading to success. We are reaping the emotional rewards that come from caring.

I always refer to Marshall Goldsmith as Mr. Generativity. Acknowledged as one of the foremost business thinkers globally, Marshall has consistently held the title of the top-rated executive coach by Thinkers50 since 2011. He has worked with top business leaders and other leadership coaches for decades.

He's developed his own method for coaching and has built a reputation and company to teach other top coaches his method. At an age when most consider retirement, Marshall decided to give back everything he built up at no cost. He posted on LinkedIn an offer to teach his coaching method to the first 15 people who responded and agreed to pay it forward. Much to his surprise, 18,000 people replied. What began with 25 coaches quickly became the 100 Coaches™ Agency, representing a spectrum of global talent from coaches to business leaders. This group of people who wanted to learn Marshall's method for free led to the formation of the company. He passes his expertise and wisdom to the top through monthly Zoom meetings, coaching workshops, in-person gatherings, and small group get-togethers with coaches throughout the year. They pass it on to their protégés worldwide through coaching and the books and podcasts they publish.

Generativity's Roots

I've used the word "generativity" several times in the chapter, but what does it mean? World-renowned developmental psychologist Erik Erikson introduced the concept of generativity to encapsulate the emotional growth and altruism that define a significant phase of our lives. According to Erikson, generativity is when a "mature man needs to be needed" (Erikson 1993). It is characterized by caring for others without expecting anything in return. Engaging in generative acts is emotionally and psychologically healthy and deeply gratifying. And it's easy. We can all engage in three forms of generativity: volunteering, philanthropy, and mentoring. I focus on mentoring because, whereas philanthropy requires giving money and volunteering to give time, mentoring is giving a piece of yourself to another to carry on something of you. It becomes a form of immortality as legacies are created, the wheels of innovation continue, and skills, values, and knowledge are passed on. When culture advances in a positive way, it is through this kind of generativity. While all forms of generativity are valuable, mentoring is the most personal and can make the longest-lasting impact. Religious beliefs, which have been passed down for centuries, are a prime example. Science, which builds on prior work, taught through mentoring, is another example. Recipes, values, and culture are long-lasting and continued because of mentorship that passes them down from generation to generation.

Generosity lies at the heart of generativity, as Stephen Post and Jill Neimark highlighted in their bestselling book *Why Good Things Happen to Good People* (2007). Giving to others is a form of self-forgiveness, contributing to overall well-being. Giving does not only benefit the receiver; individuals who engage in acts of generosity enjoy improved physical and psychological health. Generosity is often mistaken for generativity. Reciprocity is as well. I like to differentiate between the three: generativity vs. reciprocity and generosity (Figure 1.3). The breakdown is simple. If something can be generated beyond the transaction, it is generativity. Generosity is just as we know it to be: a kind gesture. An example is going to an ice cream shop, and the person behind the counter gives you an extra scoop of ice cream free of charge. That is generous. Reciprocity is a tit for tat. You scratch my back, and I'll scratch yours. There is an expectation that if you help someone, they will return the favor. Generativity is putting your expertise

Generativity vs. Reciprocity and Generosity

Mentoring Is: Generativity - Putting your expertise out to others in a nurturing and caring way

Mentoring Isn't: Reciprocity - a tit for tat

Generosity - kindness that doesn't involve generating something

FIGURE 1.3 Generativity vs. reciprocity and generosity.

out to others in a nurturing and caring way without expecting anything in return. An example is mentoring. When you mentor someone, you are generating something that was inside of you in someone else. Whether one embarks on generativity early or later in life, the positive effects are transformative, leading to lower stress levels, enhanced physical health, and a profound sense of redemption, pleasure, fulfillment, and happiness. In essence, Generativity becomes a reciprocal source of joy—a win-win scenario where one's efforts to help others also yield personal benefits.

Differentiating between generativity, reciprocity, and generosity is crucial. Acts of kindness don't capture generativity; true mentoring involves pushing a part of oneself into the world, creating something new (generating something)—a legacy. Mentoring surpasses simple favors or expecting something in return. Consider a grandmother passing down a holiday meal recipe; the generative act isn't about reciprocation but about perpetuating a legacy. I have my grandmother's Thanksgiving turkey recipe, a cherished link in my familial chain. Learning rituals and cultural traditions, a form of mentoring, ensures the passage of these practices through generations. In my kitchen, a tattered picture displays my grandmother's handwritten recipe for Thanksgiving turkey. Apparently originating from her mother, it was passed down to my mother and now to me. I pull it out every year and make the turkey for my family, intending to pass the recipe down to my children—keeping the tradition alive.

How Generativity Unfolds

Although generativity typically emerges in midlife, its timeline is fluid, much like any developmental process. Just as a baby may take their first steps at 9 or 15 months and still be considered normal, individuals may experience generativity at varying times in their lives. But the typical sequence tends to go as follows. Our 30s typically mark a period of intimacy development, where we form reciprocally close relationships with those who truly matter to us—shedding the superficial connections of earlier years (interpersonal giving to "special" others). As we transition into our 40s, a natural inclination toward generativity takes root, prompting us to look beyond ourselves, consider our accomplishments, and develop a broader concern for others. Generativity is the emotional life stage that takes up most of our adult lives.

Generativity is a transformative stage, transitioning from a potentially harried and energy-filled lifestyle to a more serene and contented mode of functioning. To be generative requires the involvement of others, and as we traverse this path, we often reflect on the mentors who have shaped us. We have been mentored in various domains such as church, sports, school, and family—unrecognized by us at times. As we switch sides and approach the role of becoming the mentor, we pass the torch to the next generation, becoming conduits for the wisdom imparted to us by mentors in previous facets of our lives.

There are numerous examples of generativity in film. Popular family movies such as *Willy Wonka and the Chocolate Factory* and the *Karate Kid* series exemplify generativity, contributing to their enduring popularity. In *Willy Wonka*, the middle-aged character, without children, seeks a successor for his chocolate factory through unorthodox mentorship and a selection process, highlighting generative themes. Similarly, the *Karate Kid* series features Mr. Miyagi, an older karate expert, mentoring a neighborhood kid, fostering a bond and mutual care. The generative theme, extending beyond martial arts, underscores life lessons. By recognizing generativity in everyday media, we can integrate it into our consciousness, facilitating a quicker and easier embrace of its positive effects.

Generativity, as I have come to understand it, encapsulates the center of the intricate journey of life. While our early and midlife years may be preoccupied with the negative facets of aging, such as physical decline and the fear of wrinkles, illness, cognitive decline, and becoming a burden, in that stage of our lives our psychological development flourishes. As our bodies undergo subtle changes—requiring reading glasses or experiencing a decrease in physical strength—our minds evolve, contributing to increasing emotional growth. The benefits of psychological development may not be immediately apparent, especially to the younger generation fixated on more tangible pleasures. However, the rewards become increasingly evident in late midlife. This is when our desire to mentor is at its peak.

Mentoring as a Form of Generativity

Mentoring is often misconstrued as a task, with the directive to "find a mentor," lacking consideration for the meaningful connection. The focus tends to be on the mentee—having someone guide the mentee up the ladder of success, neglecting the mentor. True mentorship must involve the mentor's intrinsic desire to impart their wisdom, not just the mentee's desire to receive guidance, as it is a generative process, not merely extracting expertise from someone else. Bluntly, most people are looking at mentorship backward. Mentorship comes from the mentor and is intrinsically motivated (just like we are intrinsically motivated to volunteer at a soup kitchen). This is one reason mentoring programs often fail in work settings. The perspective is on the mentee and the benefits the mentee can get, not the mentor-mentee relationship. When people tell me (and this happens *a lot*) that their mandatory mentorship programs are not working—no one signs up—it is because it is setting up the mentor to be in an *extrinsically* motivated position to help someone (just like we expect pay when working behind the counter at Starbucks). Companies set up their mentorship programs to remove the generativity component from the equation, which, in essence, is not a mentorship program but a required task involving reciprocity. The person engages in the program, and they are rewarded by their job with a better job performance evaluation, they've checked a required box, or they get paid. The goal is to have a mentee learn and advance without any thought or consideration for the mentor. These models rarely work well and, in many cases, are transactional interactions rather than true mentorship. A solution for this is to form a mentorship program based on the mentor and the principles of generativity. This creates an opportunity for a mentor to give back the way they are intrinsically motivated to. We already know the mentee will benefit from the mentorship. That is a given. Simply flip the switch.

This is what we did when we formed The Mentor Project. We made it a mentor-focused organization. I was criticized for this in the beginning, with nearly everyone telling me it would never work. I was told highly accomplished individuals (from astronauts to film producers) would not want to volunteer their time to mentor students for free. They would be far too busy, it would be a waste of their time, and they are surely inundated with people asking them for mentorship. They couldn't have been more wrong. The principles of generativity are accurate. We have a waiting list of mentors who want to join. And our mentors are world changers.

Charlie Camarda is an astronaut who flew his first mission into space on board the Space Shuttle mission STS-114. Marshall Goldsmith is the number one coach on leadership, who formed 100 Coaches, and has coached some of the world's top business leaders. Neil Comins, an astrophysicist and astronomer, has written more than 21 books. The list goes on to more than 100 experts who joined The Mentor Project. They view mentoring as an opportunity to leave their legacy, make their mark, and move the needle forward in the areas they've worked on all their lives. They are all fueled by intrinsic motivation, and pay would make them feel as if it were a job rather than a gift to themselves. Every week I have people asking to join as a mentor. For them, it is a way to feel validated, needed, respected, valued, and fulfilled. This is not the feeling most people describe when they are involved in mandatory mentoring programs in the workplace. The key to success is simple, and it doesn't cost a dime. The solution lies right under our noses. Create mentor-focused programs based on the principles of generativity and involving intrinsic motivation.

Many engage in generativity but do not realize it. It is as simple as passing family traditions to children/grandchildren/nieces/nephews. Generativity is so prevalent in our everyday lives, shown on television and in movies, that it seems to lie in the background of our consciousness. Becoming aware of generativity around us helps us to engage in it more frequently. Simply put, it is making the unconscious conscious. Once this happens, we become generative superstars in all aspects of our lives: home, work, and in the community. You've probably met some generative superstars—people who are civically engaged and involved in helping others at work and home. They are the people who are always busy and often the person everyone goes to when they need help.

How to Become Generative

As to how to become generative, don't sweat it. You probably are or are becoming generative, and you didn't even realize it! It is a natural process that occurs as you engage in activities that go beyond your identity and self-interest, developing a broad concern for others. To embrace generativity, recognize your assets and identify opportunities to share knowledge, values, and skills. Mentoring concerns involving yourself with those you like to be around and want to connect with, and doing the things you do well and enjoy passing on to others. How many times have you helped a friend solve a problem? How often have you taught a family member the holiday recipes and rituals? How many times have you helped a junior colleague or taught someone something you knew but they didn't? You were generative in every one of those instances. Mentoring, a form of generativity, is a part of our everyday lives, just like breathing air. We just don't focus on it. Imagine saying, "Breathe in . . . breathe out" all day long. We just do it instinctively. Thousands of people are mentoring friends, neighbors, relatives, and colleagues in a variety of ways. The key is to become aware of opportunities for generativity, and in this case, mentoring. Ask yourself, "What are my assets, and who can benefit from them?" Whether at work, home, or in your community, you can mentor when you connect with someone and pass on your knowledge, values, and skills. For all of you formal and informal mentors—pat yourself on the back for being generative. You deserve it!

Some quick ways to become generative:

1. Become mindful of generativity in film, TV, and media. Once you spot it, you'll see it everywhere.
2. Appreciate generativity at home—traditions, values, and culture that have been passed down in your family.
3. View interactions as opportunities to help others.
4. Reflect on your desired legacy. What is the mark you want to leave on the world?

No need to make this an overwhelming task. Enjoy the process. It is all about you. You are the star of generativity.

The Opposite of Generativity

If one doesn't reach generativity, Erik Erikson termed the outcome stagnation, a state where an individual fails to contribute to the world or others. Stagnation may stem from personal chaos or instability, resulting in feelings of lack of productivity and detachment. However, stagnation doesn't have to be permanent—we have the opportunity to reach generativity later in life. It sometimes takes longer for some to reach a stage. There are many examples of stagnation in movies. Ebenezer Scrooge, as I noted earlier, until he undergoes a transformative moment. Harvey Specter, in the television series *Suits*, is stagnant in the first season, as he is self-involved and disconnected from many relationships. There are plenty of examples in literature as well, such as Dorian Gray, the character in the classic *The Picture of Dorian Gray* by Oscar Wilde, who never wants to age, certainly doesn't give back, and rather than care for others, kills Basil, his closest friend. For all his eternal youth and wealth, he suffers from ennui. He is stagnant. As I've mentioned before, Ebenezer Scrooge is stagnant (until he has his epiphany and becomes generative). It is typical for most individuals to reach the stage of generativity in midlife.

However, it doesn't always happen in that time frame. I know someone who reached the level of generativity at 90. Joseph seemed to be in a slump for many years, just sliding by. He was retired but disengaged with friends, family, and the community. But in his late 80s, his life changed dramatically. His sister Ruth fell ill, and he took her in to live with him and cared for her with the help of aides. Joseph's once-bickering relationship with his sister became one where they sat on the couch together, holding hands and talking. Ruth's illness and need for his help was an aha moment for him that snapped him out of stagnation and into generativity. This once-disengaged man started making phone calls and inviting guests to his home. He became closely connected with his much younger, distant cousin and became a mentor to him, sharing his wisdom about social clubs and networking. His cousin's acceptance into the Harvard Club allowed him to see his values benignly passed on to his relative, with whom he became close late in life. Joseph established a legacy for himself. This successful, self-made man, who once hoarded his wealth and emotions, became a generative mentor in his final years. It was a clear transformation from stagnation to generativity. It is not unusual for someone to have an aha moment like Ebenezer and Joseph, which moves them out of stagnation and into generativity. At his funeral, at age 93, several people spoke about Joseph's generativity. His legacy lives on.

Can You Bounce in and out of Generativity?

Yes, you can. An example I like to give is to imagine a toddler learning to walk. Sometimes, a toddler will try out walking, stop walking, and then go ahead and walk again a week or a few months later (and keep on walking). We are like that, with physical and emotional stages throughout our development. Everyone reaches stages of development at their own pace. And once a stage is reached, it is normal to take a step back now and again. For generativity, an example is starting a new job. Imagine leaving a job you've mastered. You know the ins and outs and know your colleagues well and are engaged in mentoring (whether consciously aware of it or not). Then, whether by choice or not, you leave and take a new job. When you start a new job there isn't much bandwidth for anything more than getting acclimated to the new role and the new colleagues and honing your skills until you are comfortable. This is when a person may take a step back from being generative while getting the "lay of the land" at work but once acclimated, step right back into generativity. Likewise, this happens all the time in retirement. Retirement can seem deeply enticing. Then, once you leave, you are faced with "What is my identity now?" This can be difficult for many. The need to backtrack to figure out your identity outside the workplace can take you back, outside of a generative stage, while you figure things out, and then you can go right back to being generative once you have. It isn't a bad thing to move between stages. Life is fluid, and so are we.

As you can see from Figure 1.4, the stage following generativity is integrity. Integrity means that you have a feeling of wisdom and you don't have any major regrets or bitterness. Generativity helps you get to that feeling of wisdom because you have looked outside yourself and become wiser. And, as with generativity, we can move back and forth between these stages, especially in times of turmoil or change. They are fluid, and so are we.

We are naturally designed to become mentors, progressing through specific emotional stages until we feel a deep-seated urge

Stage to Reach	Failure to Reach the Stage

INFANCY

Trust – feeling safe and secure	Mistrust – feeling fear and that life is unpredictable

CHILDHOOD

Autonomy – feeling confident and secure	Shame and Doubt – feeling inadequate and filled with self-doubt
Initiative – feeling a sense of purpose	Guilt – feeling a sense of guilt
Industry – feeling a sense of competence	Inferiority – feeling a sense of inferiority

ADOLESCENCE/YOUNG ADULTHOOD

Identity – feeling of independence, control, and a strong sense of self	Role Confusion – feelings of insecurity in themselves and their future

ADULTHOOD

Intimacy – having strong relationships	Isolation – loneliness and isolation

MIDLIFE

Generativity – having a feeling of contributing to the world	Stagnation – feeling disconnected and uninvolved in the world

OLDER ADULTHOOD

Integrity – feeling satisfied with life and having few regrets	Despair – feelings of regret, bitterness, and hopelessness

FIGURE 1.4 Erikson's life stages.

to give back. This foundational understanding forms the basis of mentoring, which is characterized by unique and fluid relationships that can seem deceptively simple. However, for true mentoring to occur, certain key components must be present. Without these elements, what may appear as mentoring lacks the essence and effectiveness that define genuine mentorship. Much like our ability to age and transition between stages, our outward appearance can remain unchanged even as we undergo internal growth and transformation.

2

Five Key Components to Mentoring

The term "mentor" dates back to Homer's Odyssey, in which the character Mentor was a friend of Odysseus, guiding and counseling him. If you google the definition of mentoring, you'll be swallowed up by a long list of descriptions. These varied definitions can be confusing and make mentoring seem superficial—an activity to accomplish, like walking the dog or grabbing lunch with a friend. What constitutes a mentoring relationship is captured by the underpinnings they all share or, as I think of it, the ingredients that create a true mentoring relationship. All ingredients are required because if one is left out, it might look like mentoring, but it won't be true mentoring. Think of baking a batch of brownies. It starts with ingredients: flour, cocoa, eggs, sugar, baking powder, and oil. You mix and bake and then enjoy. But imagine the brownies if you leave out sugar. They will look like brownies but won't taste like brownies. With mentoring, if you leave out any of the five ingredients—generativity, intrinsic motivation, meaningful connections, trust, and goal setting—it may look like mentoring, but it won't feel like it.

Those five ingredients are the key components of mentoring that, when present, lead to mentoring in any situation (Figure 2.1). Let's take a closer look at each one.

5 Key Components of Mentoring

1. Generativity
2. Intrinsic motivation
3. Meaningful connections
4. Trust
5. Goal setting

FIGURE 2.1 Five key components of mentoring.

1. Generativity

Generativity is an emotional developmental stage we can expect to reach in midlife that involves caring for another without expecting anything in return. We can generally express generativity in three ways: volunteering, mentoring, and philanthropy. We may engage in all three or just one. Mentoring is an opportunity to give a part of ourselves to someone else. In essence, it is a form of immortality through the legacy we leave. Generativity is a driving force in the mentoring relationship.

In mentoring, generativity is driven by the mentor—the person giving the information, skills, knowledge, and guidance. We often think a mentee should seek a mentor, which is fine, but the mentor must come from a place of generativity. The mentor needs to want to do it.

When people who write about mentoring advise not to have a boss as a mentor because the boss will have their own agenda in mind rather than that of the mentee, they are really talking about generativity. The assumption, though, is that all bosses are not generative, and that isn't the case.

One of my first jobs was as a teacher's assistant. I moved from an office job to work at United Cerebral Palsy while I put myself through college. My boss, Kim, was the teacher. And she was my mentor. I had absolutely no idea how to work in a classroom with severely handicapped children. I was anxious about navigating the classroom and worried about how to interact with kids who were frail or who couldn't talk, walk, see, or hear. Each student had a different need, and some acted out—hurting themselves or others. When I stepped into the classroom on the first day, I was completely overwhelmed. One student pulled my hair, we had a fire drill, and I had to carry a child who weighed almost as much as me from the floor to his wheelchair across the room. I couldn't see beyond the students' handicaps to see them and their strengths. I was thinking about how to navigate the day minute by minute.

Kim stepped in and started mentoring me right away. I went to her for advice because I figured surely she could tell I had no idea what I was doing, so there was nothing to lose. It was the best decision I ever made. Kim taught me to look for the strengths in every child—even children who were really difficult. She helped me look outside myself in the relationship when working with children to see that the job of an educator is to bring the student to their full potential, not to look at each day as a series of tasks to get through. My initial instinct was to try to solve problems or to soothe. Kim taught me to try to see life through their eyes, to predict their needs so I wouldn't have to solve a problem or soothe. Once we did this we had win after win every day. And emotionally, I was so attached to each one of the kids that I would think of them outside of work (and still do today) because I could see them in a multidimensional way. The entire class had hope and optimism for each child. The kids could feel, and so could the staff. It was my favorite job ever.

Kim had a vision for her classroom. She wanted her students to succeed to their highest potential. Their success was her success. And, she wanted me, her mentee, to learn how to identify strengths in others. She understood this and articulated it so well. It was and still is her superpower. No win was too small. Even the tiniest success was to be celebrated. Kim was generative in her approach toward mentoring me. I still learn from Kim, and we remain close friends decades later. Bosses can and are often generative!

Generativity in the Workplace

Irene Yachbes started a job in a management role at a large, global company. She worked as an engineer at NASA for years, followed by a robotics company and a start-up. She was skilled at navigating jobs requiring top-notch engineering and problem-solving skills in a nontraditional, non-corporate structure. Her move to a traditional corporate job in research was intimidating. Not because she didn't have the skill set but because, like many of us at the start of a new job, she was unsure how to navigate the new territory. She was especially concerned about how the vast number of departments worked together and how to navigate them socially.

In the first couple of weeks of work, she attended an in-house event with a panel of speakers from the company. At the end of the presentation, one of the panelists, whose position was two levels directly senior to Irene, told the audience she would like to serve as a mentor. This corporate leader expressed her care about the company and those who worked there. She genuinely wanted to be a resource for others. Irene was thrilled. This was her chance to figure out how to navigate the social networks. She waited until the end of the event but, ultimately, didn't end up approaching the woman because she was intimidated. Even though the woman said she was open to mentoring, Irene worried that if she asked her for help, her vulnerability would be seen as a weakness. And this person was so high level, Irene didn't want to risk offending her in her first few weeks of work. Irene called me and asked for some friendly advice. I suggested she email her, letting her know she was responding to her talk and that she heard she was interested in mentoring someone. I also suggested Irene let her know the specific mentoring goal she had in mind so she would know what Irene was looking for in a mentor. Irene sent the email and almost immediately got a reply saying yes. The two started meeting regularly and had a great mentoring experience that continued well beyond the initial goal of getting Irene acquainted with the company layout. They even remained in a mentoring relationship after Irene changed departments. In this case, Irene's mentor let everyone in the audience know she was receptive to mentoring. The mentor initiated the relationship even though Irene asked her to be her mentor.

Irene wanted and needed a mentor at work. Generativity is the driving force of her mentor, but to the outside observer, who didn't know the full story, it might have appeared to be driven by Irene.

2. Intrinsic Motivation

Intrinsic motivation has been studied by psychologists for decades. It is a term coined by Edward Deci in the 1970s, and it refers to our drive to pursue an activity for its own sake rather than for an external reward or incentive. We are motivated to do what we love. Think about everything you would do just because it pleases you. Maybe it is reading, crossword puzzles, running, listening to music, or swimming. Whatever your passion is, you will engage in it because it brings you joy. This form of motivation is intrinsic (from within). Alternatively, extrinsic motivation is when you are motivated to do something for a reward, such as money, praise, award, or promotion; for instance, work.

In 1975, Lepper conducted an interesting study showing what can happen if you add extrinsic motivation to an intrinsic motivation (Lepper and Greene 1975). It turns play into work. The study involved preschoolers, some of whom were allowed to solve puzzles for fun. No reward for playing was offered. The other group was shown exciting toys as a reward for completing the puzzles and for doing so quickly. One to three weeks later, the teachers in the classrooms offered them puzzles without an extrinsic reward to all students. Children who had been offered extrinsic rewards (additional fun toys) in the initial experimental session were subsequently less interested in playing with the puzzles than the children who were not offered extrinsic rewards.

This happens in mentoring. The equation changes when you add an external reward or incentive to motivate someone to mentor. Extrinsic motivation becomes the driving force that sucks the passion right out of the activity we once enjoyed. For example, I ask my students to raise their hands each year if they would volunteer their time in a soup kitchen. They all raise their hands. I ask them why they'd like to volunteer to do this. After all, they aren't getting any pay, rewards, or recognition and are giving up their valuable free time. They all said they would feel good about themselves and imagined themselves enjoying the time spent volunteering, making them feel good about themselves. Then, I asked them to raise their hands if they would volunteer at Starbucks. No one raised their hand. They seem shocked that I'd ask. I tell them it is a similar situation. In both cases, people are there because they are hungry and thirsty and come to get food and beverages. The only difference is that Starbucks has an expectation of pay, which is an extrinsic motivator. Joy and pleasure differ for the two options. The joy and pleasure of providing sustenance to people was sucked out of the Starbucks option with the extrinsic motivation of pay. Alternatively, just knowing they would volunteer their time to do something worthwhile without expecting pay excited them to engage in the volunteer work even though they would be giving up their free time.

We are built to want to give back. We have a built-in intrinsic motivation, which is part of generativity. Adding extrinsic awards, rewards, and incentives to a mentoring behavior changes the dynamic and the experience for the mentor and mentee from joy and pleasure to work. The mentoring relationship can flourish when we create an environment led by intrinsic motivation.

3. Meaningful Connections

When we are adolescents, we are driven to make many connections. We are discovering our identity and need to "find our people." As we grow older and figure out our character, we slough off our superficial friendships and retain meaningful connections. Our time becomes precious with significant others, jobs, families, and responsibilities, and we don't want to waste our precious time with people who don't matter to us. As we grow older, time constraints that come with obligations don't afford us the extra hours we had when we were younger and spent hours with acquaintances. We want to spend our precious time with those who matter to us. Meaningful connections are a component of mentoring. We want to guide someone who matters to us rather than flippantly give away our skills.

When a mentor and mentee have a meaningful connection, they won't engage in a reciprocal exchange of information; they'll care about each other, and the mentee will also give to the mentor. Most of us think of mentoring as a one-way street, with all information flowing from mentor to mentee. But in reality, it is a two-way street, with the mentee providing just as much to the mentor. When a mentor knows the mentee is treasuring the information, using it, and expanding on the mentor's skills, that is incredibly valuable to the mentor. This emotional interaction is often overlooked but is very important to true mentoring. This meaningful, emotional connection is a bond that makes both the mentor and the mentee want to engage and want to help and support the other. Returning to the example of Irene and her mentor, their meaningful connection allowed them to continue their relationship beyond their initial goal. Irene allowed her mentor to see the company and the work experience through Irene's eyes and through Irene's success in the workplace, which was exactly what she was looking for. And Irene's success grew because of her mentor's guidance. It was a continuous win-win for both of them.

4. Trust

How often do you flaunt your insecurities? Probably not often. We need to trust the person we are in a mentoring relationship with. After all, mentees let the mentor know what they don't know. They are exposing their weaknesses. Will the mentor think less of me? Will an exposed weakness lead to being passed over for a promotion? Trust comes when a person feels secure in showing their vulnerabilities without worrying they will be judged. For example, you may feel uncomfortable telling someone in charge of your promotions that you have weaknesses in some areas. It may take time to feel confident enough to trust someone who has the ability to promote or fire you. One way around this is to engage in lateral mentoring™, which are mentoring relationships with people who are not your boss or in your hierarchical line. Seeking mentorship from a friend, a colleague in a different department, or someone in a different work environment altogether is a way to keep trust. When I was finishing graduate school and a fellow student was starting her externship (a required period of time being supervised in a work environment outside of the university), she was asked to calculate a statistic called kappas, which is used to measure inter-rater reliability in qualitative research. We were both in the same program in the same year, and I just happened to remember how to calculate this form of statistical analysis. We didn't have the advanced statistical programs we have today, so this was a big deal. My fellow student had no idea how to do them but didn't trust telling her new boss that she had absolutely no idea how to calculate them. So she called me. She knew I'd calculated kappas before and could probably teach her. Truth be told, I had been in the same boat with other problems plenty of times and called her for help. This time, when she called, I was happy to help. We sat on the phone and worked it out in about 20 minutes. She solved the problem while learning how to calculate them and completed her first big work problem. She trusted me, knew I would not judge her and could help guide her in a time of need.

To summarize, mentoring requires trust, and that can often be difficult in hierarchical situations. A great solution is to engage in lateral mentoring™.

5. Goal Setting

Mentoring requires a goal. Just walking up to someone and asking them to be your mentor without any inkling of what you'd like to be mentored in rarely works. In the case of Irene, it was to understand how the company worked—to get the lay of the land. In the case of my fellow student, it was to learn how to calculate a statistic that could solve her work problem. In both cases, the mentor understood the goal and was able to provide guidance. A mentor can also set a goal. In Irene's case, her mentor had a goal to mentor someone on workplace issues—helping people understand how the large corporation operated. Setting a goal helps a potential mentor or mentee know whether this is a good fit for them and provides the opportunity for an outcome. The mentor and mentee need to know and agree upon goals. Clarity leads to success, while a lack of goals leads to meaningless meetings, resulting in a lack of results.

In reflecting on effective mentoring, these five key components illuminate the path toward robust mentorship relationships. While it is conceivable for mentorship to exist without one of the five components, the strength and depth of such relationships inevitably suffer. Understanding the intricate interplay between these components is paramount for individuals embarking on either side of the mentoring journey—whether seeking mentorship or aspiring to become mentors themselves. Furthermore, organizations that cultivate thriving mentoring programs should look to these foundational elements to foster meaningful mentoring programs. The modern, digital forms of mentoring should also be considered. Just as we have found ourselves in a much more online world, mentoring has taken a step in that direction as well.

It is worth acknowledging that imperfect mentorship, lacking in some components, can still offer valuable insights and growth. After all, some mentoring can be better than no mentoring! However, the full spectrum of components within the mentoring relationship enables us to go beyond the simplistic portrayal of mentoring as a mere passing of knowledge from mentor to mentee. Instead, it uncovers a complex dynamic full of opportunities for mutual growth and education.

Too often, disappointment sets in when mentoring falls short of expectations. These disillusionments often stem from overlooking the complex nature of mentorship. It is not a static arrangement but rather an evolving relationship that demands nurturing and commitment from both parties involved. As we contemplate our own mentoring experiences, assessing the presence of these key components helps us create a multidimensional mentoring relationship. Should we find ourselves lacking in some areas, it is an opportunity for introspection and growth. Perhaps by identifying and addressing these gaps, we can breathe new life into our mentorship endeavors, or alternatively, seek out alternative avenues better suited to our needs and aspirations. In some cases, mentoring may not be what we need. Embracing the complexity of mentorship and the richness offered by these five components, we open ourselves to a journey with intentionality, knowing that each component holds the potential to enrich and elevate our mentoring experiences, both personally and professionally.

3

What Mentoring Isn't

Imagine someone you know throws out the term "mentor" about something that is happening in their life. As they talk further, do you soon realize you're not on the same page? The term is often used casually in everyday language, inadvertently diminishing the true value and significance of mentoring and the relationships it entails. It's a refrain heard far too often: people claiming (often sincerely) to be mentors when, in reality, they are not. Among the myriad misconceptions surrounding mentoring, one of the most prevalent is the conflation of advising, networking, sponsoring, and coaching with mentoring itself, or the belief that mentoring is merely a subset of these activities. However, mentoring stands apart as a distinct practice; not only is mentoring separate from these activities, but each of them is separate from each other.

The danger of equating all these roles with mentoring is that true mentoring fails to materialize despite the parties involved believing otherwise. This confusion not only hampers the potential benefits for both mentor and mentee but also diminishes the standards and expectations associated with mentoring and other related practices. In essence, blurring these distinctions is not only misleading but ultimately detrimental to fostering genuine mentoring relationships and reaping their full rewards.

An Advisor Is Not a Mentor

An advisor has comprehensive knowledge or specializes in an area and uses their expertise to help others grasp challenges that may come up and understand the goals and needs they may have.

Advisors and mentors share similarities in their roles of providing guidance and support. The advisor role can be mistaken for a mentor because, in addition to guidance and support, they have experience in their respective fields, which they use to assist their advisee.

Advising Is an Obligation

Professor Joel Weinberger teaches psychology at the undergraduate and graduate levels at Adelphi University. In addition to teaching classes and writing scholarly articles, as part of his job as professor of psychology, he is required to advise undergraduate and graduate students. As he explains it, advising is an obligation. It is in his contract, and he has to do it. Undergraduate students typically come in to see him once a semester with a list of courses they want to take. While they can do this online without his advisement, he is available in the event they would like to meet. Generally, they ask Professor Weinberger to approve the list of courses they come to him with because they are the courses the student would like to take. In most cases, this is an easy task because the classes presented to him are classes that fall within the correct amount and type of courses the student is supposed to take. Once in a while, he will have to point out to them that they need to take certain courses that are not on the list of courses they've presented. Sometimes, he thinks that they are overdoing it, taking too many courses, and they will not be able to carry that course load. Alternatively, they may not be taking enough courses. Once in a while, students have a question about which of two courses to take, both of which would fulfill the requirement to graduate, and based on past courses they've taken and what their goals are, he helps them choose which course to take. But the real job is just to make sure they get through the program and take the courses they're supposed to take, and if they run into a problem with a professor or with a course, they can talk to him.

The role of student advising is fulfilling a job requirement, and the time and energy that's put into it depends on the needs of the student. The role of advising students in the clinical psychology PhD program is more involved because the students are not just picking courses. Here, the role of advisor is much more time intensive. Dr. Weinberger meets with his students as a group weekly and often one-on-one in between. In the PhD program, the advisors are not assigned. Instead, students choose their advisors, and the professors they choose must agree.

Dr. Weinberger's advisor role is not to sign off on courses or help choose the courses the students take, as it was with the undergraduate students. In the graduate program, the students must take courses in a certain sequence and a specific number of courses each semester. Their schedules are preset. He needs to advise them through a research project, which is called a second-year project, in which they must present their research findings at a conference or publish them in an academic journal. Following the second-year project, the advisor's goal is to help the students to complete their dissertations. In addition to helping the students choose their dissertation committees, Dr. Weinberger provides his expertise in research to help them design and carry out their dissertation projects. Beyond that, they can individually come to him with whatever personal issues they have in the program. The advising ends when they pass their final PhD dissertation defense. At that point, if the advisee and Dr. Weinberger wish to remain in contact, his role changes to that of a senior colleague because there is no longer a specific set of requirements that he needs to advise them through. He may also become a mentor at this point, guiding them through whatever they need or working on projects together.

Dr. Weinberger mentors students from time to time after they graduate. Valentina Stoycheva was a student who transitioned from advisee to mentee after graduation as she continued to seek guidance and advice about her career and her desire to write. Joel received an offer to write a book about the unconscious, a topic he is an expert in. His time was extremely limited, but he wanted to write the book. He asked his now mentee, Valentina, to coauthor the book with him. She agreed. Joel guided her through the process. She contributed in a legitimate collaborative manner to the content, but Joel, who had experience authoring books, helped her with the expectations, organization, timeline, contract, and other nuances of writing a book. As the process moved forward, she also began to take on some of these duties. Their book, *The Unconscious*, was published in 2020. By the end of the project, Valentina knew enough to work on a book of her own if she so chose. Joel now refers clients to her, and their role has shifted yet again, this time from mentor/mentee to colleagues.

An advisor is often mistaken for a mentor because there are many similarities. However, as we can see in the example of Dr. Weinberger, the advisor role was an obligation. He was required to advise students as part of his job. Advising students is an extrinsically motivated interaction rather than intrinsically motivated one, as it became when Dr. Weinberger moved from advisor to mentor with his former student, Valentina. His extrinsic motivation to advise her changed to intrinsic motivation when he became her mentor, and they wrote a book together. He also took on a generative role because he wanted to help her advance her writing and asked her to coauthor a book with him. Valentina was learning from Joel, and his legacy now lives on through her in her deeper understanding of the unconscious and writing.

Another difference between mentor and advisor is the presence of a meaningful connection. Although meaningful connections happen with advisors and advisees, that isn't always the case. The undergraduate advisees may never even meet their advisors because they can sign up for their courses online and may simply email for advising. In the case of graduate students, a meaningful connection is more likely because the advisor and advisee have worked together regularly for several years. This is where mentoring and advising can become confusing. The difference is whether the role is required as part of the job, which means it isn't an intrinsically motivated interaction. In that case, it is advising rather than mentoring.

In other settings, such as work, what may seem to be mentoring may actually be advising. If the job requires mentorship, even if it is an informal requirement but is expected, it may actually be an advisor role instead.

Advisors are appointed or assigned formally where there are structured guidelines and expectations (as with course assignments, graduate school requirements, and work-related goals). Mutual interest and compatibility are not always present in advisor-advisee interactions as they are in mentor-mentee interactions.

The role of the advisor is often temporary, just long enough to complete a goal, and the role is generally hierarchical. Mentors and mentees may have longer relationships because of their deeper connection, and their relationship is often lateral rather than hierarchical. While both advisors and mentors play vital roles in guiding and supporting others, there is also an important difference. Those differences lie in the areas of motivation and generativity. Mentors are engaged of their own volition, without pay, reward, or awards, and their goals are to help the mentee to grow and develop because they care, without expecting anything tangible in return. They are acting intrinsically, through generativity.

A Sponsor Is Not a Mentor

A sponsor is someone in a position of influence or authority who actively advocates for and supports the career advancement of another person. Sponsors use their influence and networks to create opportunities, open doors, and promote their protégé's visibility and advancement within an organization or industry. They are instrumental in helping protégés secure new roles, projects, promotions, and other career-enhancing opportunities.

An example of a sponsor in the business world is a senior executive who takes a proactive role in promoting and advocating for the career advancement of a talented individual within their organization. A CEO would be considered a sponsor if they recognized the potential of a high-performing employee and actively supported their promotion to a leadership position. They may do this by endorsing their protégé's abilities, providing visibility, and/ or recommending them for key projects or opportunities.

A well-known example of a sponsor is Oprah Winfrey, a powerful sponsor for many individuals across various fields. Through her influential platform, Oprah has helped launch the success of authors through Oprah's Book Club. She features their books and introduces them to a wide audience. She sponsored Dr. Phil McGraw, now known as "Dr. Phil," through his numerous talk-show appearances on the Oprah Winfrey Show. Dr. Mehmet Oz got a significant career boost and television show after appearing on and being promoted by Oprah. Suze Orman also gained prominence after receiving endorsements from Oprah and appearances on the Oprah Winfrey Show. Her sponsorship has propelled the careers of numerous talented individuals in the literary, media, and entertainment industries.

I've had several sponsors. The Mentor Project would not have started without Jim Moriarty reaching out to his prominent friends who he knew valued mentorship, introducing me, and promoting my work to them. After I spoke with Jim about mentorship, he said, "I've got a few people you have to meet." He made email introductions and phoned others he thought could help me. He even contacted Senator Chuck Grassley's office (they didn't respond). Jim's sponsorship was instrumental in my career. I met and connected with founding members of The Mentor Project because of Jim's sponsorship.

Jennifer Snow is a retired Lt. Colonel and former intelligence officer with the Air Force. She has been in charge of as many as

10,000 people when deployed. She has been an instrumental sponsor for me. When we had only 10 mentors, she brought me to an entire day of meetings in New York City to meet people who could help scale The Mentor Project. From noon til 9 p.m., I met with her industry contacts. She also made phone calls to leaders with a passion for mentoring, and within six months, we grew from 10 to 60 mentors. She has also been my sponsor as a member of the board of directors for The Mentor Project for the last four years. Her guidance and advocacy have helped me to understand leadership. She has helped me advance my career by increasing the visibility of my work on The Mentor Project, and she has advocated on behalf of the organization to help us secure board positions, grant opportunities, and mentors in various tech fields.

Similarities between sponsors and mentors are that both provide support, guidance, and advocacy. These are intrinsically motivated. Unlike an advisor, whose job is to guide their protégé, sponsors advocate because they have a desire that is not motivated by pay or other extrinsic motivators.

The differences between sponsors and mentors are that sponsors primarily focus on advancing their protégés' careers by providing strategic opportunities, visibility, and connections. Conversely, mentors focus on providing guidance and support across personal and professional development, although they may also open doors for their mentees. Mentors also have an ongoing relationship with their mentees, whereas sponsors may have infrequent but highly influential involvement when it comes to providing career-boosting opportunities. Sponsors tend to have career-focused goals, whereas mentors have a more holistic set of goals that cover personal and career goals for their mentees.

Sponsors and mentors are frequently used interchangeably, especially in work settings. However, it is important to distinguish between the two because their goals are different, and outcome expectations of the person being sponsored versus mentored should not be the same. Both sponsors and mentors guide and support, but the goal of the sponsor is to advance their protégé's career through strategic opportunities and advocacy, whereas the goal of the mentor is to take a broader approach to personal and professional development. Mentorship can include sponsorship, but sponsorship does not include mentorship.

Networking Is Not Mentoring

Generally speaking, networking refers to exchanging ideas, information, interests, and services with people who share a common interest or profession. It is cultivating productive relationships for business or employment through a supportive system of exchanging information. It can take place in a variety of settings, such as informal events, social gatherings, online platforms, and networking groups. Networking allows people to communicate ideas, connect, collaborate, and build professional and personal connections. It can play a crucial role in career development and opportunity. There are a myriad of personal and professional organizations that help people connect and network. These include Facebook, LinkedIn, BNI (Business Networking International), MasterMind groups, chambers of commerce, the Rotary Club, and Kiwanis.

Networking serves as a window into the lives of those within our social or work circles. It encompasses everything from learning about social happenings (think of Facebook) to the latest trends in our professions (think of any professional networking organization). The raison d'être of anyone engaging with these organizations is to harness these connections, become or stay relevant, and/or end up with more business or social interactions.

As stated above, people engage in networking through various avenues. A few of the most popular online and in-person examples are highlighted below.

Online

LinkedIn is a social networking platform designed specifically for professionals and businesses. One of LinkedIn's primary purposes is to facilitate professional connections. Users create profiles that function as digital résumés, highlighting their skills, education, work experience, and professional achievements. Users can connect with colleagues, industry peers, potential employers, and clients. LinkedIn has more than 990 million users as I type this, with more than 65 million business and 150,000 school accounts (Iqbal 2024).

Meta (Facebook) is a personal social networking platform. Facebook allows users to connect with friends, colleagues, acquaintances, and people with shared interests. These connections form the basis of networking by providing opportunities to interact, share information, and build relationships. There are also Facebook groups and Facebook pages, which bring together people with common interests, professions, or goals, which can lead to networking. Facebook has more than 3.59 billion core users as of 2021, according to statista.com (Dixon 2024a).

Instagram is a social media networking platform focused on sharing photos and videos. Instagram's visual nature, engagement features, and community-driven environment make it a powerful platform for networking, brand building, and establishing professional connections across various industries. Users create profiles where they can upload photos and videos, apply filters and editing effects, add captions, and tag locations. Instagram's direct messaging feature allows users to initiate conversations, collaborate, and build relationships with other users, including potential clients, collaborators, influencers, or industry peers. According to statista.com, Instagram has more than 1 billion users worldwide (Dixon 2024b).

In Person

Business Networking International (BNI) is the largest referral networking organization in the world, with more than 12 million referrals made in 2023. It is a professional referral marketing program whose goal is to create long-term professional relationships through in-person meet-ups.

Chief is an exclusive professional networking organization of more than 10,000 women executive leaders. Networking happens through meet-ups, a vetted Rolodex, masterminds (a peer-to-peer mentoring group of experts who help members solve problems), and workshops.

Entrepreneurs' Organization (EO) is a peer-to-peer networking organization with more than 16,000 entrepreneurs globally. This nonprofit aims to bring entrepreneurs together through collaborative learning and access to top business leaders.

Think of networking as a resource-gathering endeavor. It provides us with connections, valuable information, and learning opportunities. Remember the old-fashioned Rolodex? It sat on desks, ready to connect individuals, call upon contacts in times of need, and propel business forward. Networking operates the same way, virtually and in person, with the Rolodex of individuals replaced by organizations.

How Networking Is Different from Mentoring

Networking is reciprocal and/or generous rather than generative. Networking aims to make connections that help you gain in work or socially. Although networking can lead to some meaningful connections, the ultimate goal is to make connections that will elevate your business or social opportunities. Networking does not meet all of the key components of mentoring: (1) generativity, (2) intrinsic motivation, (3) meaningful connections, (4) trust, and (5) goal setting. Networking does have goal setting and trust and, in some cases, meaningful connections, but it lacks generativity and intrinsic motivation. Networking is about expanding your network of connections, whereas mentoring is about personal growth and learning from someone with more experience. This is the case even in lateral mentoring™, with the caveat that the mentor is not in a position of power.

Fred Klein is the cofounder of Gotham City Network. He's 82 years old and has had a lengthy career as a labor lawyer in New York. Fred is the ultimate networker. Just mention anyone's name, and he will pull his phone out, scroll for a minute through his photos, and then present you with a photo of him with the person you just named. It is like a parlor trick, except it is real. Networking is in Fred's blood. But he is also a prolific mentor. Fred is a mentor with The Mentor Project, and I am proud to say he mentors my 18-year-old son, Aiden Weinberger. My son attends Fred's alma mater, Syracuse University, and is an athlete, like Fred was, and he guides Aiden in the fine art of networking. Aiden wasn't his first mentee. Fred has been mentoring for decades. He believes in combining mentoring with networking. He teaches his mentees the importance of meeting people, forming relationships, and building a modern-day Rolodex.

How Networking Can Lead to Mentoring

Fred interacts with almost everyone he meets. It is as though networking is in his DNA. One day, back in the early 1990s, he went to a camera store to develop some film he shot. Fred did what he does everywhere he goes. He struck up a conversation with Vincent Pugliese (Vinny), the guy developing the film. As a master networker, Fred's goal is to get to know people beyond a superficial level and see where he can fit them in the Rolodex inside his brain. He asks questions such as, "What high school did you attend?" and "What do you see yourself doing in ten years?" He doesn't bother with questions such as "How's the weather"? Fred frequented this film developing store, and each time he returned, he'd learn more about Vinny. It turned out that Vinny graduated the same year as Fred's son Alex and from the same high school that both Fred and his son attended. Fred was cooking with gas now; his networking juices were flowing. He had a solid place to put Vinny in his networking Rolodex—he had a personal connection, and with each bit of information he gleaned from Vinny, his information card grew. Fred was 59, and Vinny was 29 when they met. Fred's son Alex had already graduated from law school by this time, whereas Vinny was working at a film developing store. Fred's empathy kicked in. He wanted to help this young man, so over time, his relationship changed from networking to mentoring.

Vinny was not a good student in high school. He didn't want to be there except for the social aspects. His claim to fame in high school was skipping art class nearly 90 times and still managing to pass the class. Vinny knew how to charm his way by talking with his teacher in the hallway. The year after Vinny graduated, the school changed their attendance policy.

Vinny wasn't sure he was going to make it to graduation. Just days before graduation day, when all of his friends were talking about and preparing for the colleges they were going to attend in the fall (Hofstra, Harvard, Tufts, Yale, etc.), Vinny was waiting to hear whether he would be walking for graduation or attending summer school. He couldn't even register for the local community college because he wasn't sure he would be a high school graduate. It turned out that Vinny did graduate. But he didn't go to college. He got out and "screwed around" for four years. He got arrested. He stole from his job every day. Not because he needed what he stole but because he could. He gave everything he took to his friends and explained that he didn't have scruples. His moral barometer was low. He didn't have anyone mentoring him; his family life was not the best, and he was basically living life without any guidance. Basically, Vinny was looking for and getting into trouble.

Vinny eventually entered community college, had six majors over several years, and never finished. While working at a place called Dairy Barn, he stole a little money from each customer by overcharging them just enough so no one would notice. He moved back in with his parents right around the time everyone else was moving out of their parents' homes. In Vinny's own words, he was a loser. One day, his conscience kicked in. He woke from a nightmare of an older woman shaking her finger at him, telling him she'd come for him for stealing money from her.

Vinny decided to try the one thing he liked but never took a chance on: sports photography. He loved sports and figured that although he wasn't athletic, he could probably take pictures. His first job in his new life as a straight citizen was working at a film-developing store. He bought a camera and tried to figure out the rest of his life.

This is when Fred entered Vinny's life. Just when Vinny needed someone to take an interest, just when he finally started living life by the rules, Fred started coming by the store to develop his film. Once Fred and Vinny developed a relationship and discovered commonalities in their lives, Fred took it upon himself to trade his networking hat for his mentoring hat.

While conversing as Fred was picking up his photos, Fred asked Vinny what he planned to do in the next five years. Vinny said he wanted to be a photographer. Fred told Vinny to give him a port-folio. He'd show it to a friend of his who was a sports manager. Maybe he could use Vinny as a photographer. The next time Fred stopped in, Vinny handed Fred his portfolio. For the better part of a year, Fred peddled the portfolio to his network to no avail. He came back to the store with the bad news. He'd exhausted his network. Fred told Vinny that he wasn't a loser for working in the photography store and trying to find his dream job. But, as he walked out the door, Fred said, "If you are still here in five years, you are a loser."

This struck Vinny like a speeding car hitting a brick wall. Vinny mentioned this moment as a pivotal moment in his life. It changed him. He valued Fred and the mentorship he'd been giving him and really wanted to make sure he wasn't in the camera store in five years. Shortly after this, he quit his job and turned his life around. He had one image in his head—Fred coming in to see him working there in five years. It horrified him, and he told himself, "Fred will not come back here in five years and see me working here." That motivated him to quit the job. He didn't have a backup, but he knew he ran the risk of staying in the job because it was easy to do, but he couldn't risk Fred's disappointment. He booked a ticket to Chicago and went from stadium to stadium, taking pictures. He used his networking skills (and skills he learned to ditch class in high school without consequences) to get into games and to the front row, and he continued to work to get his foot in the door.

Vinny got his big break in what could be a made-for-television storyline. He was at a game with his camera and saw a guy on the sideline walk toward him. He leaned down to Vinny, who was taking pictures, and asked whether he would be his assistant for the day. His own assistant didn't show up for the game. This was Vinny's dream job—an NFL photographer. Vinny was given a press pass and, on that day, his life changed. He got a fantastic picture of a touchdown pass, which was the beginning of his 22-year career as a professional photographer.

Years later, Fred heard from Vinny, who contacted his son Alex to get Fred's number. He called Fred to tell him he had made it. He wrote about Fred and talked about Fred on his podcast. But he hadn't told Fred personally. When Fred heard how Vinny turned out and that he had been a valuable mentor to him, nothing could have made him feel better. That is the ultimate reward for a mentor. Your mentee made it!

Vinny is now known as Vincent, and this former successful photographer of more than 20 years is now a successful entrepreneur and author. His unstructured past has been replaced with the security of a loving family and a thriving network. In fact, he is known for creating memberships for companies and individuals. What better way to utilize a network? Fred's mentorship rings loud and clear in Vincent's life decades after his film-developing days.

I met with Fred and Vinny together over Zoom to talk about this story, at Fred's request. This was another way of Fred solidifying relationships and networking. Of course, Fred made sure to find our mutual connections, and, as it turns out, we had more than 50 mutual contacts on LinkedIn, and our interests intersected in many areas. Vinny plans to join The Mentor Project.

And it's all thanks to Fred's networking, that deepened to mentoring and changed the trajectory of Vinny's life. Vinny is fulfilled in his chosen field.

Networking can be mistaken for mentoring because it has the look and feel of lateral mentoring™. Two experts coming together to help each other out. The difference is that networking has a goal of personal gain rather than to help the mentee gain. The generativity piece is missing. Networking is a unique connection that is not hierarchical as advising, coaching, and sponsoring are, but it is still not mentoring. Rather, it is a lateral connection that can lead to lateral mentoring™. And that is just what happened between Fred and Vinny.

Coaching Is Not Mentoring

Coaching is focused on achieving specific goals or outcomes. A coach's approach is structured and goal-oriented. A coach works with an individual (coachee) to help them achieve a specific personal or professional goal and is generally explicitly hired for that purpose. They have expertise in methodologies for working with clients in various areas, such as leadership development, career transition, and personal growth (and sports).

Marshall Goldsmith is one of the world's top-ranking executive coaches. He developed the Stakeholder-Centered Coaching method, a structured process that focuses on improving an individual's performance and leadership abilities within an organization. His method helps leaders achieve positive, long-term, measurable changes in behavior.

In his long and successful career, he's coached notable leaders, including Alan Mulally at Boeing, JP Garnier at Glaxo SmithKline, as well as other CEOs and senior executives at major companies. His work focuses on feedback and guidance based on confidential 360-degree feedback from colleagues and sometimes friends and family. This is a proactive method that involves setting specific goals and skills in the service of improving. The feedback is used to further those improvements and gain insight to develop leadership skills and reach predetermined goals.

Coaching is often mistaken for mentoring. I recently gave a talk to a group of more than 100 coaches on mentoring. Many of the coaches said, "Coaching is mentoring." I asked if they would continue working with their clients if they were not getting paid. The answer was an emphatic no. I asked if they (the coach) benefited in any way from the coaching experience outside of getting paid. I asked whether the coachee's success was a legacy for the coach. Did the coaching make them feel they would be willing to help and care about their coachee's outcomes without expecting anything in return from them? For each question, the answer, again, was almost always no.

Mentoring differs from coaching in that mentoring pulls from intrinsic motivation, personal wisdom, and expertise. Mentoring is not a structured, standardized interaction between individuals. There is a personal connection that drives the relationship forward that does not necessarily focus on measurable changes in behavior but rather provides support and guidance. An analogy I use is that mentoring opens doors for the mentee, whereas coaching is focused on getting the coachee to open the door themselves. Marshall Goldsmith agrees. "Coaching and mentoring are both valuable tools for personal and professional development, but they serve different purposes and are structured differently." Guiding, opening doors, and providing insight do not always equal mentorship. We all engage with others, often in meaningful ways. We also engage laterally, but coaching is a hierarchical-only method of interaction between coach and coachee. Mentoring often involves mentors who are not in a vertical relationship but are seen as equals with differing areas of expertise. When coaches mistake coaching for mentoring, they rarely see mentoring as complex. Mentoring is a web of connections rather than a superhighway.

Our motivation for connecting with others matters. Are we connecting to get ahead? Are we connecting to get paid? Are we connecting because we want to pass on our knowledge and leave a legacy? The outcomes we seek for ourselves matter. It is vitally important that we look at the five key components of mentoring to determine whether or not we are meeting the criteria for mentoring. Sometimes, it may look or feel like mentoring, but it may be something else.

While advising, sponsoring, networking, and coaching are all valuable practices in their own right, they are distinct from mentoring. It's crucial to leverage each of these practices to their fullest potential. However, we must also recognize and separate them from mentoring and from each other, to avoid missing out on the unique benefits that mentoring offers. True mentoring enables mentors to share their insights and ideas with mentees in a way that sparks transformative change. By embracing the distinctiveness of mentoring, we unlock its power to ignite meaningful growth and development.

We've demystified what mentoring isn't. Now let's unravel a deeper question: Why do we mentor? What drives us to invest our time, energy, and wisdom into nurturing those who walk alongside us on their journey? Buckle up, because we're about to delve into the purpose behind our pursuit of mentoring.

4

Why We Mentor

A s documented in world scripture, the message is the same across major religions. One thing people of many faiths seem to agree on is that giving is good. Christianity (Luke 6:38), Buddhism (Garland Sutra 21), and Hinduism (Bhagavad Gita 17 20–21) advocate giving as a central principle. Christianity—Give, and you will receive; Buddhism—Enlightened people give generously, giving without regret, without expecting a reward, and without seeking honor or material benefits. They help all living beings. Hinduism—Give because it is right to give. Giving without expectation is enlightened giving. Giving with expectation is selfish giving. Similarly, Judaism (Mishnah about 4.1), Islam (Koran 39.10), and Taoism (Tao Te Ching 17) all speak to the benefits of kindness, faith, and honor toward fellow man. Judaism—He who honors mankind is honored. Islam—Those who are kind will have kindness. Taoism—If you don't have faith in others, others will not have faith in you.

Culture and religion have valued giving back since time immemorial. The term "mentor" dates back to Homer's *Odyssey*, in which the character Mentor was a friend of Odysseus (actually Athena in disguise), guiding and counseling him. The character Mentor can also be traced to the book *Les Aventures de Telemargu* (translated as *The Adventures of Telemachus*) by Frances Fenelon, published in 1699. In this book, Mentor from The Odyssey travels with Telemachus as his tutor. More recently, President John F. Kennedy famously stated, "Ask not what your country can do for you, but what you can do for your country."

Mentoring is most often associated with jobs or career growth, but it is much more than that. Mentors have long guided mentees through paths of safety, relationships, and spiritual growth. Dr. Christopher Bellitto is a professor of history at Kean University in New Jersey. He specializes in the Middle Ages and Church history and has published five books on the Church, spirituality, and the Bible. One of his favorite mentor-mentee relationships in the Bible is that between Ruth and her mother-in-law, Naomi. In fact, Dr. Bellitto argues that the Old Testament Book of Ruth ought to be renamed The Book of Naomi because the mentor in the relationship was Naomi. Had Naomi not mentored her daughter-in-law, neither may have survived, and their legacies would have been lost.

Survival: The Book of ~~Ruth~~ Naomi

The book of Ruth starts with her mother-in-law, Naomi. Naomi is married to Elimelech, and they have two sons, Mahlon and Chileon, who are married to Orpah and Ruth. The family lives in Moab, which neighbors the land of Judah. Naomi, her husband, and her sons hailed from Judah, whereas Orpah and Ruth are native to Moab. Naomi's husband dies, and then her two sons die. This is a big deal for the surviving three women. They could starve. There is a famine in Moab. Women were not safe without the protection of a husband, so these were particularly difficult times for the three women. Naomi decides that her best bet is to return to her native land in Judah, whereas it would be best for her daughters-in-law to remain in Moab. And this is what she counsels them to do. Orpah does, but Ruth refuses. She stayed with Naomi, and they went together to Bethlehem, in the land of Judah, to stay with relatives at the beginning of the barley harvest because Naomi hoped that they'd find food and a better life there.

Ruth knows little about life in Bethlehem. She was a foreign woman in a foreign land. Naomi took Ruth under her wing and mentored her. They were both widows in a tenuous situation in a patriarchal society. Naomi and Ruth demonstrate devotion to and protection of one another in order to survive. Out of the depths of their sadness, Naomi noticed a kinsman named Boaz who was looking at Ruth. Naomi went into mentor mode and told Ruth to catch his eye but not appear too eager. Their lives were on the line, and Naomi and Ruth both understood the importance of securing a husband for Ruth. Naomi advised Ruth on how to get and keep Boaz's attention, and eventually, Boaz and Ruth got married. Naomi was mentoring her daughter-in-law in a social situation that changed both of their lives. They moved from potential starvation to a legacy that had enormous consequences in The Old Testament. The legacy began when Boaz and Ruth had a son named Obed. Naomi was so excited to become a grandmother that Naomi's friends would say Ruth didn't have a baby boy; Naomi did. This baby was mutual security for them both. Ruth and Boaz had another son, Jesse, who then had a son, David, who became king. Yes, that King David. The greatest king in the history of ancient Israel and the prophesied ancestor of the Messiah.

Some might say that Naomi's mentoring was self-serving. The Bible clearly does not think so. Naomi's mentorship of Ruth led to the birth of David, a pivotal figure in both Judaism and Christianity.

Spiritual sources offer examples of mentorship that reflect many of the same issues we see in modern life. The sentiments for mentoring often have a similar theme: we need to give back, with our own desires fueling the relationship.

I've already discussed how we are built to mentor and detailed the five components of successful mentorship. But there are also some reasons people desire to mentor that make the experience valuable and often life-changing. When we align our built-in need to give back with our own desires, mentorship can be downright magical.

Most people have a desire to generate something that moves beyond themselves into another person or the world. Like Naomi, who mentored Ruth to a new life and lasting legacy, when mentors move an idea beyond themselves, it is powerful regardless of whether you are a widow facing starvation or a CEO of a powerful organization. This is how we make meaning in our lives and how we express generativity. Whether you are an innovator or a grandma, you have taken in an enormous amount of information in your life; you have accumulated knowledge, skills, and values. You are a precious natural resource and library of information! Most people do not opt to keep their experience and wisdom to themselves but instead choose to share them with others. The desire to do this comes through in many ways. Among them are the need to feel useful/helpful, feel validated, and leave a legacy.

To Feel Useful

Throughout our lives, from toddlerhood to older adulthood, we all have a desire to be useful. Toddlers follow their parents around, "helping" with everything they see their parents doing. Whether folding the laundry or picking up toys, they jump into action as little helpers. It helps them feel confident in themselves and to become more autonomous. As teens, usefulness is often directed toward academics and extracurricular activities as a way to demonstrate their own values and skills. Feeling useful and needed helps young adults transition to adulthood as they seek to develop their identity and place in the world (Fuligni, Smola, and Al Salek 2021). Adults feel useful by providing for and raising their families, volunteering, mentoring, and caring for others. The feeling of mattering is important to older adults. Mattering, as a term, is in the same category as useful and needed. We feel that we matter when we perceive ourselves as useful and needed. It is a protective role that makes us feel important to others, which can provide a buffer against loneliness and physical decline as we grow older (Flett and Heisel 2020). According to van Vliet, feeling useful is essential even for those who are suffering from dementia (van Vliet et al. 2017). The study revealed that adults suffering from young onset dementia, like their non-demented counterparts, have a desire to feel useful. Engaging in activities that helped them feel useful was found to be critical to their well-being.

Being involved with others and in meaningful activities helps us feel secure and balanced. The alternative, uselessness, can have significant negative effects on children, teens, and adults. Emotional effects such as depression, anxiety, and feelings of worthlessness can result from feeling useless. Poor coping strategies can result in extreme negative consequences, including substance abuse, weight gain, or even self-harm. From as early as we can remember, all of us have a desire to be useful. We want someone else to see what we do as important to them.

When Bill Cheswick told me he was retiring, he had a lot of great things happening in his life. He and his wife Lorette bought a farm, their children were launched and doing well, and his financial status was better than he had expected. All of his boxes were checked. Bill was a success. But . . . he didn't feel useful.

Bill started his career with Bell Labs in 1987. Bell Labs was an engineering think tank, arguably the best in the country. Ten Nobel Prizes have been awarded for work that took place there. They are credited with developing the laser and the transistor, among many other inventions. Bill was in his element. He experienced his work environment at Bell Labs as an intense playground of innovation. He thrived there. He pioneered much of the information technology work, which led to several patents. He played a crucial role in developing innovative methods for searching and retrieving information from the vast company network, which was particularly important in the early days of computers when data management was still in its infancy. His contributions spanned various technological areas. He and Steven Bellovin created one of the world's first network firewalls. They coauthored the first book on this topic, *Firewalls and Internet Security,* where they described the framework of the network firewall still in use today. Nowadays, we take the security we have when typing an email, banking online, making purchases, or doing a basic search for granted, but this was brand-new territory when Bill helped create it. While at Bell Labs, he also started the Internet Mapping Project, which allowed companies and the government to map their Internet use. The photos of early Internet mapping look like beautiful Rorschach inkblot art.

Bill never worked in a silo. He was always teaching colleagues what he knew, and at the end of every year, his boss required an "I am Great Sheet" from the team. Every person in his workplace was required to write down all of the accomplishments they'd been part of during the calendar year. It was a documentation of usefulness. Like most people there, the years flew by for Bill as he and others moved from project to project. This yearly "usefulness" task helped Bill (and likely everyone else) see how much he accomplished and how relevant he was to the company. You really can't get more concrete than an annual report of your usefulness! One of Bill's rewards for his usefulness was to give public talks about his work. They were, essentially, putting his "I am Great Sheet" on public display, letting the world know about the new innovations he'd been creating. He was useful and relevant in the workplace and around the globe.

While still at Bell Labs, Bill (his friends affectionately call him Ches) cofounded Lumeta, a company focused on developing fiber optic components for telecommunications. He stayed with this groundbreaking company for 12 years before returning to AT&T (formerly a part of Bell Labs) and then retired in 2012 to a farm in New Jersey. He went from high-speed usefulness to slamming into a brick wall. How do you go from world-changing innovation to spending 24/7 on a farm? Gone was his annual "I am Great Sheet." He couldn't find his usefulness and, therefore, his relevance.

What to do?

It was right around the time of Bill's retirement that we met. I interviewed him about mentoring, and it was at this time I learned how useless he felt. His life looked picture perfect: a brilliant, loving wife, amazing adult children, a gorgeous farm, and money in the bank. But his tank was empty. He was at his best when teaching others and helping to solve big problems. Bill wanted to teach elementary school-age children quantum mechanics, but no kids were around. It wasn't like he could go to a park to ask kids, "Hey, wanna learn wave-particle duality?" People would probably have thought him nuts.

Bill lit up like a Christmas tree as he talked about teaching kids science and math. He asked me to imagine fourth graders having fun with science before they become jaded and think it is too hard or boring to pursue. I could see the excitement on his face through the Skype screen (this was before Zoom took over the world) at feeling useful again. It wasn't that he wanted to go back to work. He needed to feel needed and useful in a new way. When Bill retired, he lost his daily interaction with his peers and, thus, his relevance. His enthusiasm for solving problems and innovating was bottled up on the farm, and he needed to receive the external validation that we all crave, and that comes from being useful.

It took a few years, but we got Bill and some other science, technology, engineering, and math (STEM) mentors into a home-school co-op in New Jersey, a middle school, a Girl Scout troop on Long Island, and a high school in the Bronx. The spark was reignited in Bill. He was back! Bill would hop in his Tesla and drive hours to meet with kids all over the tri-state area. His usefulness cup was full. And, his relevance returned.

Kids loved Bill "Ches" Cheswick. Wednesday became "Ches Day" at the homeschool co-op, The children enjoyed his mentoring so much that they wrote him cards; one student made him a rocket sculpted out of beeswax. There was so much success and pleasure from mentoring that it led to the creation of the organization The Mentor Project™, which was incorporated in 2019. Bill wasn't the only one feeling useful. All of us who volunteered—Jura Zibas (our lawyer), my dad (artist, web developer, and mentor), Bill Cheswick (mentor), Gabriel Lewis (education outreach), Bob Cousins (mentor), Irene Yachbes (mentor), and myself (CEO and mentor)—felt useful and relevant.

Just six months after incorporating, COVID hit. The world shut down, and Bill was back on his farm and back to his old feelings of useless irrelevance. We pivoted, and moved to Zoom lectures and meetings, and while not the same as in person, it was better than nothing. As the world began to open again, Bill had mentors and mentees visit his farm. A new spark was ignited. Bill found a high school student to mentor one-on-one. The mentee's work output skyrocketed, and the two formed a close bond, even after the student went to college. They remain in regular contact today, several years later, and Bill says he feels his mentee is now more knowledgeable than he is in the areas he helped him in (Bill is notoriously modest). Bill's mentee took his expertise, expanded upon it, and moved it forward. The mentoring relationship infused usefulness and relevance back into his life. It's important to Bill that he is useful and contributes to the world. He finds he gains relevance through sharing his knowledge and mentoring others.

Many people lose their feeling of usefulness when they transition to retirement. The tasks at hand are not deemed useful or worthwhile, which can shake a person's well-being. It is like having a honey-do list every day. We don't always find mundane daily tasks relevant or useful to our well-being. But there is a readily available solution. Projects we choose that we would do without pay (based on intrinsic motivation) can afford us an opportunity to be relevant and infuse us with a sense of usefulness. Mentoring provides a sense of usefulness and relevance. It can lead to what psychologists call flow. "The best moments usually occur when a person's body or mind is stretched to its limits in a voluntary effort to accomplish something difficult and worthwhile. Optimal experience is thus something that we make happen" (Csikszentmihalyi 1990).

To Feel Validated

All of us have the desire to be worthy, to belong, and to have positive self-esteem. We seek validation in order to experience these deeply rooted psychological and social dynamics. One way we evaluate ourselves is through feedback from others. When others tell us we are doing a great job or we are doing something meaningful, or are successful, we feel validated. We feel that we are part of a group, we are good at something, or we matter to others.

Validation is how we measure ourselves when we set standards for our accomplishments. We seek feedback from others to help determine whether or not we've achieved our goal. At work, we need our coworkers and bosses to validate our work so we can feel that we are part of a team and we are successful in our work. It feels great to have a positive performance review.

In our social lives, we seek validation to see how we fit in with others socially. We seek validation when we want to know, "Do others like me?" or "Am I a valued member of my community?" When someone tells us we are a good friend, or if we get recognized in our house of worship or our neighborhood, we feel validated. We are social beings, and validation helps us feel that we belong and are worthy members of society and relationships.

Validation is also a foundation for mentorship. It is a strong motivator. We are motivated by the desire to be validated, and we are also motivated to validate others. In a mentoring relationship, a mentor validates their mentee every time they show they care. Guiding through sharing knowledge, values, and expertise are all forms of validation. When a mentor takes time from their day to focus on their mentee, it shows that they find the mentee worthwhile and that they belong. This validation acts as fuel, igniting the mentee's intrinsic motivation. Mentors, in turn, feel validated by their mentees' successes and by seeing how much they matter to them. The validation between the mentor and mentee is a major driving force in keeping the mentoring relationship alive.

The Writer

Alan Zweibel always loved comedy. In the late 1960s, when Alan was in college at the University of Buffalo, he'd hole himself up in his dorm room during the long, brutal northern New York winters writing jokes. Then he'd mail them to Johnny Carson and *MAD* magazine to see whether any would get accepted. He got a lot of polite rejections. But then he noticed that a lot of the monologues on late-night TV started having jokes similar to his. Alan didn't think they were stealing from him. Rather, he felt that this showed that he had something to offer. This validation carried him forward because he knew he was on the right track. His jokes were on par with the A-list professional comedy writers.

Alan described the fear he had following his graduation from college. His friends went off to medical school, law school, and dental school while he moved back in with his parents to work in a deli. Alan's future was filled with uncertainty, which he was reminded of every time someone asked him, "What are you doing?" He still found time to write and occasionally sell his jokes, however. They sold for $7 a joke to comedians who worked in the Catskill Mountains, in upstate New York. Each sale was a validation for him.

Alan always remembered his struggle to break in as a comedy writer. The uncertainty, the questioning of others, were difficult. But when a joke did sell, the struggle was worth it. The greater the struggle, the more validated he felt. He wanted others to have this experience. Mentoring became natural for him, because he wanted to help others who shared his love of comedy writing.

Alan's success began in his 20s. He was one of the first people to write for *Saturday Night Live*. He was there from the beginning, writing for people who became iconic, such as Gilda Radner. It's hard to keep track of all the places he's lived and worked because he has been busy ever since his career took off in 1980. One thread that has been consistent throughout his long career is that he works hard, holds meaningful friendships for decades, and has always craved validation. He consciously knows he needs validation. How else can he know whether he is doing well at his craft? Imagine telling jokes in a closet to yourself. How long can a person in the entertainment industry operate without validation? Not long, I'd wager! Alan also knows that he needs to validate others. It is what grounds him.

Giving back through mentorship has been important to Alan since he got his job at *Saturday Night Live*. Alan met his wife, Robin, shortly after he started working there. She was part of the production staff. She always made sure to help Alan feel special. Every time a letter came to the show from a kid who said they wanted to be a comedian, Robin would make sure the secretary put Alan's initials on it so that it would go directly to his desk. Robin knew Alan loved to give back, and this gesture was part of their early dating—providing Alan the opportunity to give back. And he did. He answered all of the letters. Even though he considered himself to be very lucky, he also knew what it's like to struggle, and he remembered every person who was ever nice to him. He had a lot of mentors through every phase of his career, and as soon as he was able, he wanted to do the same for others. Each letter validated him and reminded him that he had made it as a comedy writer.

Those years of giving back have had a payday more valuable than any cash, award, or applause. Throughout all phases of Alan's career, he received letters and emails thanking him for answering their letters and mentoring them. Some have stopped him on the street to thank him. He moved from the East Coast to the West Coast and back more than once, and every now and then, when he and Robin are packing and unpacking, they'll come across a letter from a decade or more ago thanking Alan for his mentorship.

One letter sticks out. Somewhere around 2010, Robin came across it in a move from LA to New Jersey. The letterhead was from a radio station at a high school on Long Island, New York, and was dated October 1983. It was addressed to Mr. Zweibel, thanking him for getting on a train in a snowstorm in New York City to go to a town on Long Island to be on a student's radio show. The student made a vow that if he ever made it, he would remember Alan's example. That student was Judd Apatow. For those of you who don't know, Judd is a renowned comedian, director, producer, and screenwriter. His list of accomplishments is too long to detail here, but a few of them include The *40-Year-Old Virgin*, *The King of Staten Island*, and *Anchorman: The Legend of Ron Burgundy*. The list goes on and on. The letter Judd wrote to Alan is framed and hanging in Alan's office today. Talk about validation.

Alan didn't just help Judd when he was a teen in high school. Judd knocked on Alan and Robin's door when he was just starting out in comedy. Alan took the opportunity to mentor Judd, and as he gave him a tour of his brownstone in Manhattan, he showed Judd the pictures of him on the walls with all the famous folks he was writing for. Alan shared the phone numbers of Al Franken and Rodney Dangerfield to help Judd break into the comedy writing field. When Judd was asked on talk shows about how he got his start, he was able to reflect on his visit and Alan's mentorship. More validation!

Alan and Judd have remained friends, and their relationship moved from Alan as the mentor and Judd as the mentee to a lateral mentoring™ relationship. As Judd progressed in the field of comedy, Alan was no longer the sole mentor. Once Judd became a recognized name, he started mentoring Alan from time to time. Now, they validate one another.

Research shows that validation is associated with a sense of belongingness and self-esteem, which are essential to well-being (Maslow 1958). Abraham Maslow was a psychologist who theorized that human motivation was based on a hierarchy of needs. The hierarchy is based on five stages:

1. **Physiological needs:** These are the most basic needs for human survival and include food, water, shelter, and sleep. A failure to meet these needs can negatively affect an individual's physical well-being and functioning.

2. **Safety needs:** Once physiological needs are met, individuals seek safety and security, which includes physical safety as well as financial and health security.

3. **Love and belongingness needs:** After safety needs are satisfied, people seek love, affection, and a sense of belonging. This includes relationships with family, friends, and romantic partners, as well as membership in social groups and communities.

4. **Esteem needs:** The need for esteem includes both self-esteem and the esteem of others. Self-esteem involves feelings of self-worth, self-respect, and confidence; the esteem of others involves recognition, respect, appreciation, and validation from others.

5. **Self-actualization needs:** The final stage of the hierarchy is self-actualization, which is the realization of one's full potential, personal growth, and the fulfillment of individual aspirations and goals.

Stage 4, esteem needs, involves the desire for recognition, respect, and validation from oneself and others. We are built to need validation. Fulfillment of esteem needs are essential for our psychological well-being. The alternative may be feelings of inadequacy, low self-esteem, and a lack of motivation.

Intrinsic motivation is also a key component in mentoring. Validation serves both the mentor and the mentee. It fuels an intrinsically motivated mentoring relationship. Validation is a two-way street, with a need to be recognized and appreciated by others as well as a need to recognize and appreciate others. When Alan describes mentoring, he says it is part of his "core." And the core of mentoring for him is feeling validated and validating others.

To Leave a Legacy

More than 25 million individuals are in the DNA database of Ancestry.com, the world's largest digital consumer family history resource (Ancestry n.d.). As of 2024, there are 60 billion online records, with roughly 1 billion searches made monthly. We get deep satisfaction from spending hours learning about the history of our lineage. More than 131 million family trees have been created on ancestry.com alone. This doesn't count the census and other genealogy sites and resources. Legacy is built into how we think of ourselves.

How Do We Understand This Need?

We don't just crave the legacy of our lineage. We also want to know that we made a difference in the world. An examination of 17 articles concerning the priorities of palliative care patients as they neared death revealed legacy as an increasingly crucial factor in their thinking (Von Post, Wagman, and Wagman 2017). Legacy served as a connection between life and the prospect of death, helping these patients come to terms with their imminent mortality. The impetus to create a legacy stems from both altruism and a longing for enduring significance, striving to be remembered beyond the confines of illness. The aspiration to leave behind a legacy provides a sense of empowerment. It helps us shape our sense of self, similar to how our familial heritage contributes to our self-understanding.

Organizations also recognize the significance of leaving a lasting impact. In a 2023 article featured in HR News, a 50-year-old articulated his aspiration to transform the human resources field to prioritize empowering employees for excellence over personnel management tasks (Horowitz 2023). This is how he expressed his yearning to establish a meaningful legacy in the workplace. Rather than simply fade into retirement, a legacy in the workplace holds immense value for many individuals. Most people simply don't realize that leaving a legacy in the workplace is an option, or if they do, they don't know how to proceed. Given that the workplace consumes a substantial portion of our time, attention, and cognitive resources, it naturally serves as a platform for showcasing our skills and expertise. We strive and yearn for our contributions to make a meaningful difference. Crafting a legacy allows us to sustain relevance even after transitioning into retirement.

Legacy is important to all of us as a way to remain present after we are gone (from work or life). Mentorship presents itself as a potent avenue for leaving behind a legacy. Whether within the professional sphere or in our personal lives, a legacy endures beyond our direct involvement. And it matters.

Is There a Way to Measure Mentorship as a Legacy?

The answer is *yes*, with a legacy tree.

Imagine a family tree, but instead of relatives, it depicts your mentors and mentees. The beauty is its ability to transcend familial ties; it doesn't matter whether we hail from royalty or humble beginnings or have a rich or modest lineage. We possess the agency to chart our own path. We select those we wish to be mentored by, position ourselves within the tree, and extend its branches to encompass those mentees whose lives we have touched. In doing so, we construct a narrative of our own making that holds greater significance than mere genetic inheritance.

It wasn't until I sat down with Dr. Robert Lefkowitz, the 2012 Nobel Prize winner in chemistry, that I learned about a legacy tree. Bob has mentored more than 200 people over the past 50 years. Leave it to a Nobel laureate to figure out how to categorize and organize his relationships over the decades. He understood the concept of DNA legacies and didn't hesitate to expand that concept to mentoring.

In 2018, Bob published a truncated version of his legacy tree in an article he titled "The Serendipitous Scientist" in the scientific journal *Annual Review of Pharmacology and Toxicology* (2018). This contribution was simple yet profound. His legacy tree, a map laid out just like a family tree, consisted of everyone who mentored him in his career and everyone he mentored. Each generation was linked, just as in a family tree.

Bob titled the article "A Serendipitous Scientist" because of the serendipity of his becoming a scientist. As a young boy, he aspired to become a physician, not a scientist. As he wrote the article, he pondered how he shifted from being a physician to becoming a Nobel Prize-winning scientist.

He started by thinking about the people who mentored him. His memories took him all the way back to the Vietnam War. He was part of a cohort of young physicians who were drafted during that war, referred to as Yellow Berets. This was a take-off on the idea of Green Berets, our most courageous Special Forces (the name Yellow Berets jokingly connoting cowardice). During the Vietnam War, there was a lottery draft for all men over 18. But for physicians, there was no lottery; everyone was drafted into one of the military branches or US Public Health Service. A draft into the military could result in a year in Vietnam. However, for the Public Health Service, there was also the possibility that you would remain stateside and be assigned to a government research institution such as the Centers for Disease Control and Prevention (CDC) or the National Institutes of Health (NIH). Bob was assigned to the NIH, where he spent two years. He was one of about 100 physicians each year who were sent there (with little or no training). In total, there were roughly 800 physicians over the years. Remarkably, of those, 10 went on to win a Nobel Prize. Let me repeat that. Despite no previous scientific training or aspirations, 10/800 of physicians assigned by the armed forces to the NIH went on to win a Nobel Prize. Remarkably, in Bob's class (1968-1970), 4 of them went on to win the prize. That was 4% in his group! Bob mad an interesting side note that Anthony Fauci (he calls him Tony) was also in his class. While he didn't receive a Nobel Prize, he reached a very high level. How could this be?

Bob wondered the same thing. How could so many physicians, with little to no training, become Nobel Prize winners? And he was one of them! A light bulb flashed. It occurred to him that there are commonalities among the family branches if you look at family lineages. Families have the same DNA, so they look alike and have similar characteristics. He reasoned that if you look at people's lineage but swap out genetics for scientific lineages, he could map out those 10 Nobel laureates. He could map out who trained them, who they trained with, and who they trained. He began by looking at those who trained under the 10 Nobel laureates as scientific children or scientific grandchildren of one of the Nobel laureates. Then he looked back two generations before those 10 Nobel laureates and added those individuals. He created a "scientific family tree" showing a clearly delineated scientific lineage of the 10 Nobel laureates. He referred to it as the legacy tree (Figure 4.1). Bob found the mode of transmission for all of the "scientific DNA" that connected the scientists was mentoring.

Bob didn't stop with the diagram. He wondered what made the mentoring successful for this "scientific family." As he pondered this, he realized that the students (or mentees) apprenticed themselves to their mentors. The mentors guided them to pick the best problems to try to solve, and the mentors were models of how to push on in the face of repeated failure. Day in and day out over a period of years, the mentees would learn from their mentors how to make decisions, remove distractions, and push toward goals. That isn't something that can be learned from a manual or a classroom. It needs nurturing and modeling over a long period of time. It needs mentoring. Bob likened the mentoring relationships to learning as an apprentice would, rather than by lecturing and explaining as in a typical classroom setting.

Bob's own legacy tree started with his two mentors when he was at the National Institutes of Health. He worked equally with both of them, and they were both physician-scientists. Their names were Jesse Roth and Ira Pastan. Bob considered himself fortunate because each mentor had different strengths and weaknesses. In a way, they were polar opposites of one another. One mentor was creative; the other was modulated and critical. Both were necessary to Bob's success. He needed to have creative ideas cultivated and then to have them put into practical terms so that he could work to solve a problem successfully. His two mentors brought a balance to his way of thinking and operating. He took the creativity and enthusiasm of Dr. Roth and the critical and rigorous approach of Dr. Pastan to navigate his career as a scientist successfully.

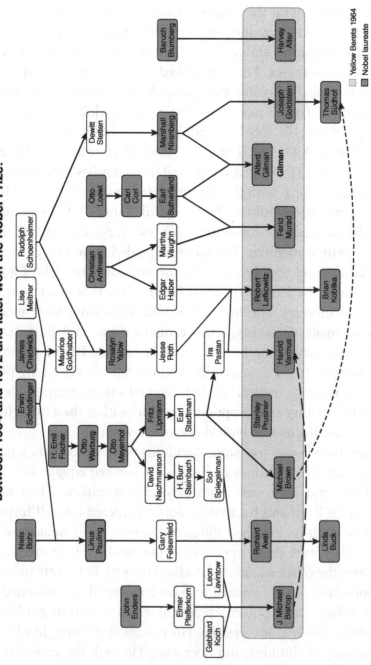

Scientific lineages of the ten Vietnam-era Yellow Berets who trained in research at the NIH between 1964 and 1972 and later won the Nobel Prize.

FIGURE 4.1 The legacy tree.

Bob folded this approach to science from his mentors into his own thinking, as any good apprentice would. He then paid it forward by passing his way of thinking onto his own mentees. One mentee who is prominent in Bob's memory and on his legacy tree is Brian Kobilka. Bob was Brian's mentor, helping him develop his scientific skills the same way his mentors taught him. This mentoring relationship was so successful that in 2012, they were jointly awarded the Nobel Prize in chemistry. Mentor and mentee shared the award! The pride Bob feels about this is tremendous. A mentee's success is exactly what every mentor strives for, and Bob was able to share the ultimate level of success with his mentee. There are roughly 200 other mentees Bob has worked with, and he can talk about the accomplishments of many of them with the pride a parent would have when talking about their child's achievements. They are all part of his legacy tree.

Bob attended a professional conference not long after publishing his article about the legacy tree. An attendee approached him excitedly and proclaimed, "I'm a sixth-generation Lefkowitz, and I wanted to introduce myself." Bob was puzzled, but the person told him he read his article, saw the legacy tree, and realized his mentor was five degrees away from Bob on his legacy tree. Bob's great, great, great, great, great scientific grandchild explained the research he was doing, and to Bob's amazement, he could hear the work that he'd worked on with his own mentees expanded upon by this person he'd never met. Bob brimmed with satisfaction and fulfillment, and his pride was through the roof. Simply put, the people Bob trained went on to train others, and so on. He saw his legacy played out in real time right in front of him.

Most people won't have a legacy tree littered with Nobel Prize winners, just as most people don't have a family tree brimming with royals. Nonetheless, it is satisfying to reflect upon our ancestry and see whether we can find traces of ourselves in our heritage. Similarly, it can be fulfilling to reflect upon those who guided us and those we've mentored to see whether we can find traces of ourselves in our mentoring heritage.

Rather than just highlighting pedigree, the legacy tree shows how you matter. It shows your imprint on others and the ripple effect of your impact extending well beyond one person. You can consider it a butterfly effect. Just as with a family tree, where you may never have met your great-grandfather, you may have his nose or another feature that you've carried on. In the case of a legacy tree, a part of each mentor is carried on to the next generation and develops into a second, equally important "family." Dr. Lefkowitz explained that his legacy tree is as essential to him as his family tree, and he is excited and proud of his mentees when they achieve, just as he is with his five children.

We spend enormous amounts of time at work and with colleagues. But how many people spend time reflecting upon their mentors and mentees? How often do we reflect upon the effect of our work? Or how our mentors influenced our work and how we affect the lives of our mentees? Most of us don't spend time reflecting on our work pedigree. Years can go by without a thought to the process and, at retirement, it is easy to feel that our work is over. But it may not be. Our ideas and expertise continue in our mentees, their mentees, and their mentees after them. It is a form of immortality. It is a legacy often undeclared, unrecognized, and rarely celebrated. But it should be.

The simple act of mapping out our mentor lineage allows us to absorb the magnitude of the work we accomplish and its impact on the world. It shows how we fit into the world. Just like the family tree, the legacy tree illuminates our contributions. It goes well beyond our résumé, well beyond titles and LinkedIn profiles. It shows that we matter and that we will continue to matter.

When mentors are able to give back in the way they want, and to whom they want, they can change lives, leave lasting legacies, and change the surroundings of themselves and their mentees. There is no person who cannot mentor another. There isn't a person who cannot leave a legacy. Those who don't have a chance to mentor can face anything from a lack of a sense of safety to the loss of a legacy. We all want to feel that we matter in life. This was captured beautifully in the classic film *It's a Wonderful Life*. In this movie, George Bailey (brilliantly played by Jimmy Stewart) discovered how much he mattered to his family and community. He had an important and profound legacy. This movie resonates with all of us because we all have the same desire to matter and leave a legacy. Mentorship can provide this for us.

Why do we mentor? It's more than a mere transaction; it's a value we hold dear. Mentoring reveals our purpose and motivation—the driving force behind our engagement in these transformative relationships. We mentor for myriad reasons and in myriad ways. Some styles are deliberate choices, while others emerge organically from our interactions. The next chapter delves into these diverse mentoring styles, illuminating the rich tapestry of strategies and techniques that guide our mentoring practices and foster meaningful connections.

5 Mentoring Styles

Mentoring isn't a one-size-fits-all relationship. There are several styles of mentoring, leading to limitless possibilities of connecting with others for personal and professional growth. Most people think of mentoring as hierarchical, but there are other forms as well: peer and lateral mentoring™. When we access all forms of mentoring styles, we expand our impact potential with each and every interaction.

Hierarchical Mentoring

Hierarchical mentoring is the conventional view of mentoring. When most people think of mentoring, they automatically think of traditional, vertical mentors, i.e. those who are older and more experienced. Think master and apprentice. Most also think of the mentee as the sole beneficiary of the mentor-mentee relationship.

Hierarchical mentoring is most like an apprenticeship. A mentor imparts their skill to the newcomer. For centuries, apprenticeship was a way to keep a craft or trade going. It was a future job opportunity for the apprentice and a legacy for the "master" of the craft or trade. Both parties are meaningfully connected, with

67

benefits coming to both. They both gain from the experience. We still have apprentices in trades, but they aren't as common as they once were.

Internships have taken the place of apprenticeships in many settings. Students, recent graduates, or individuals transitioning to new positions can intern. But there are distinct differences. Mentorship focuses on long-term personal and professional development (as does an apprenticeship), with mentors providing guidance, support, and advice based on their experience and expertise. An internship, on the other hand, focuses on gaining practical work experience in a specific field or industry. Interns generally work on projects, tasks, or assignments under supervision in order to learn skills.

Hierarchical mentoring is most often found in organizations that have a "ladder" to climb. Examples are corporate, health care, and academic settings. In personal life, hierarchical mentoring is often carried out by grandparents or other relatives, teachers, community organization leaders (scouting, sports, hobbies), and religious/spiritual leaders. In these cases, a mentor is in a higher-level position, mentoring someone who is inexperienced or younger and therefore lower in status. Think of hierarchical mentoring as a two-lane highway or a ladder. No turns. Just one direction.

Many individuals believe that hierarchical mentoring represents the sole form of mentoring that exists. Further, we are typically taught to seek mentoring in this conventional, hierarchical manner. This is the form of mentoring that is most often confused with other forms of guidance: advisors, sponsors, and networking. This is because the potential mentee usually drives hierarchical mentoring. The mentee wants to get something or go somewhere. In some cases, they are looking for someone to open doors for them or to give them something they need without any desire for a relationship or to give something back to the mentor. I think of it as someone looking to pluck an apple from a tree. They need or want something, and they seek to take it. There isn't anything negative in this, but as mentioned in a previous chapter describing what mentoring isn't, hierarchical mentoring is often viewed as an opportunity rather than a relationship.

Hierarchical mentoring works best when a mentor is imparting their expertise or wisdom to someone who is receptive to it. The mentee then does something with this new knowledge or skill. What is often not emphasized or even recognized is that the desire to mentor must be present in the mentor. The relationship must be a two-way street. The mentee must want to accept the knowledge and put what the mentor is imparting into the world. There must be a goal, and the connection between the two must be without external rewards and meaningful to both.

Reverse Mentoring

Reverse mentoring is a form of hierarchical mentoring, because it is mentoring in one direction. In the case of reverse mentoring, however, the mentor is the newcomer or younger individual and the mentee is the "expert" or more senior individual. An example of this is a grandchild mentoring a grandparent in navigating new technology. In the workplace, this is someone who is lower on the hierarchical ladder, mentoring someone higher up in something they are more knowledgeable in, such as technology or communication styles used by younger generations.

The relationship is still hierarchical, but the roles are reversed. Often, hierarchical mentoring involves reverse mentoring as the relationship between mentor and mentee develops. An example is *The Karate Kid*, with Daniel, who is being mentored by Mr. Miyagi in karate, but he is also mentoring Miyagi. Throughout their relationship, Daniel provides emotional support to Miyagi. He encourages Miyagi to confront his past and reconnect with his roots in Okinawa, showing that mentoring isn't just about teaching skills but also about emotional and personal development.

Lateral Mentoring™

Lateral mentoring™ involves working with mentors who might be the same age, younger, or even in a completely different field. The key is that lateral mentors™ help us expand and open up the creative potential of where our ideas can go and how our connections can be built. Lateral mentors™ also tend to engage in small acts of mentorship that often lead to high output.

We engage in lateral mentoring™ all the time, and we often don't even realize it. Think of all the times you've engaged with someone to solve a problem, advance an idea, or get clarity from someone to add to the work you've already done.

The five key components of mentoring explained in Chapter 2 are the same for lateral mentoring™ (Figure 5.1). There is no difference in the key components for any form of mentoring. The only difference is that we are seeking mentorship from someone who is not hierarchically above us.

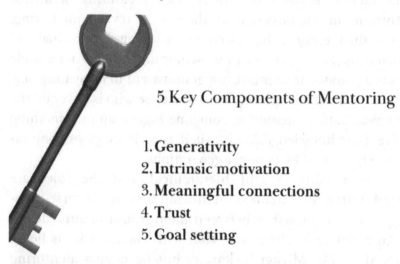

5 Key Components of Mentoring

1. Generativity
2. Intrinsic motivation
3. Meaningful connections
4. Trust
5. Goal setting

FIGURE 5.1 Five key components of mentoring.

The benefits to the mentor are the same in lateral mentoring™ as they are for hierarchical mentoring:

• Productivity

- Legacy
- Purpose
- Connectedness with the larger community and the world
- Deep, meaningful relationships
- Better physical and emotional health

The benefits to the mentee are the same in lateral mentoring™ as they are for hierarchical mentoring.

- Knowledge
- Expertise
- Career guidance and goal setting
- Increased job satisfaction
- Personal and professional growth
- Skill development

How Lateral Mentoring™ Differs from Hierarchical Mentoring

Lateral mentoring™ enhances the purpose for the giver and receiver. It creates a new kind of "community" in a world that has tended toward being hyper-individualized. We've become accustomed to individualistic problem-solving and climbing a ladder with either no help or some help from those above. Lateral mentoring™ expands our vision to include parallel support and guidance. This is very helpful to us because lateral mentoring™ is inherently less pressure-filled. The mentor-mentee relationship is focused on the solution of the moment rather than on an abstract future goal. We can utilize lateral mentoring™ in any setting, from home to community to work. We can find our lateral mentors™ virtually anywhere. Simply look left and look right. You may be looking at your next mentor.

Classmates as Lateral Mentors™

For the past couple of years, I've had the privilege of teaching courses in the Psychology Department of a university, teaching introduction to psychology, child development, the psychology of gender, and the psychology of prejudice. Most of the classes include a substantial writing component, requiring three APA style papers. APA style is a cornerstone of scholarly writing in the social sciences and involves meticulous guidelines for formatting and citation.

My students range from freshmen to seniors, bringing a wide spectrum of writing skills to the table. For some, writing in APA style comes naturally, while for others, it's a daunting task that triggers considerable anxiety. In one particular course, this disparity was stark: nearly half the class excelled at APA writing, while the other half struggled significantly. The first set of paper submissions highlighted this issue, with grades split sharply between high achievers and those who fell short of the mark. This was concerning because mastering APA style is crucial for psychology students, many of whom aspire to attend graduate school.

Determined to bridge this gap, I discussed available resources with the class. I emphasized the benefits of the university's writing center, encouraged students to schedule one-on-one time with me, and introduced the concept of lateral mentoring™—seeking support from fellow classmates. The response was immediate and inspiring. One student, who had been struggling, received an offer of help from a classmate right after our discussion. They arranged to meet outside of class. Another student approached me afterward to say she planned to seek guidance from a friend who was a strong writer. This spirit of lateral mentorship quickly spread through the class.

By the time the second papers were submitted, the improvement was noticeable. Students who had struggled initially showed significant progress, and overall, the class's writing performance improved. The atmosphere of mutual support not only enhanced their writing skills but also fostered a stronger sense of community. Students began studying together and continued to offer and seek help from one another.

This experience underscored the power of lateral mentoring™ in academic settings. Each classroom has students with varying degrees of comprehension. The subject matter is irrelevant. In a stats class, some students find the coursework easy while others struggle. In writing classes, some students soar while others have difficulties. In my classroom, I was able to see lateral mentoring™ transform the students from individual units who didn't communicate with each other into a collaborative environment where students not only improved their writing skills but also built connections.

This is lateral mentoring™, and we all engage in it all the time.

How many times have you asked a friend to help you with something because you trusted them? How many times have you consulted with someone? Perhaps it was with a friend; perhaps it was a hallway conversation or a conversation over lunch. Many of these kinds of interactions lead to lateral mentoring™. Why? Because we trust people who are lateral to us. They aren't threatening to our jobs or to our role. This is especially true when we don't want to be seen as vulnerable in front of someone hierarchically above us. This kind of mentoring can be with family, work, or community members.

Friends and Family as Lateral Mentors™

Charles Camarda is a NASA astronaut who flew his first mission into space on board the Space Shuttle mission STS-114. His mission was the first "Return to Flight" following the Space Shuttle *Columbia* disaster, in which the shuttle disintegrated, killing all astronauts on board.

Charlie grew up in a tough neighborhood in Queens, New York, with immigrant Italian grandparents on both sides of his family. They were hard workers who came to this country to provide a better life for their children and their children's children. Charlie's parents instilled values in him: family, faith, and friends. He grew up with those values, and they shaped his life. He internalized doing the right thing for your family, not embarrassing your family, and being honorable. These moral codes were the foundation of trust and psychological safety that were critical for him because his surroundings weren't always safe. He learned to fight and push himself to do things he was afraid of. He taught himself how to swim by jumping off the diving board into the deep end of the pool rather than telling his friends he couldn't swim, and he rode the A train (the subway) to Brooklyn Polytechnic High School every day, which wasn't a walk in the park academically. His values were helpful to him in overcoming challenges because it helped him develop his group of trusted friends, family, and colleagues, all of whom he calls upon for mentorship in times of need. This group of friends constitutes his lateral mentoring™ network. They are from all aspects of his life. He has had this kind of lateral mentoring™ network since he was a child because his family encouraged him to trust family and friends.

Charlie called his trusted group of family and friends his Friends of Charlie (FOC). Some of his childhood friends are still on his FOC, but he continued to build and grow his network, adding new trusted people as he moved through life. This has come in handy for him, especially at work. When you are an astronaut, your life depends on an entire management team. It was hard for Charlie to find great hierarchical mentors, because he didn't trust that he could speak his mind and be taken seriously because of the hierarchical bureaucracy. He didn't believe people would or could speak freely if they felt something was not right. But he could always rely on his FOC. He knew they had his best interest at heart, and he trusted them with his life, literally. He always relied on his FOC for mentorship while he was working in very hierarchical environments. This lateral network helped him solve epic challenges. It is his lateral mentoring™ "little black book" of people whom he can call on when he needs mentorship.

Charlie even took his FOC lateral mentors™ into space, just in case he needed their help. I'm not sure whether he literally brought a book with him on the shuttle or he memorized its information, but he made sure he had the ability to access his lateral mentors™ when he was in space. That's because Charlie didn't really trust the leaders who were launching him and the other astronauts into space. After all, the previous mission had ended in catastrophic disaster. His list is everyone he trusted in NASA and everyone outside NASA who would tell him honestly if something wasn't right—even if they thought it would be upsetting to him. He knew that if there was a danger in space, he could call on them, and they would guide him.

These individuals were people he'd grown to trust over the years. He built a trustworthy and multilayered network of people who have ties to multiple other people in other areas. This bond enables him to build on the trust of his inner circle to expand his network. Trust is a key component of mentorship, and trust can often be missing in hierarchical environments. Charlie mastered his small-world network and built it out beyond his inner circle. As Charlie explained, "When someone in your network doesn't know someone, your trusted friend will send you to their trusted friend, and then you know that person has the same standards your friend had." He thinks of this as a personal social network, just like the big social networks, except each person is trusted. His "little black book" of lateral mentors™ was thick as he prepared for space. Some were personal friends whereas others were valued colleagues who he trusted implicitly with his life.

When launch day came, Charlie had his FOC with him. And once in space, as he feared but came prepared for, there was a problem. A problem that could have been fatal. A piece of material was sticking out from the bottom of the spaceship in the shuttle orbiter near the nose region. The managerial team on the ground wasn't sure whether anything needed to be done to fix it before returning back to Earth. Charlie called upon his lateral mentors™ to get their advice. They were people he had worked with at NASA Langley, and he trusted them. He didn't go through Mission Control. Instead, he called his lateral mentors™ from space. His mentors told him the crew needed to fix the problem before returning to Earth. It would require an unrehearsed, unplanned emergency spacewalk to make it happen. The team on the shuttle (not Charlie) made the spacewalk, and it was determined they wouldn't have made it safely back to Earth if they hadn't made the repair. Their shuttle could have had the same fate the previous mission had. Lateral mentoring™ literally saved them.

Charlie's crew in space operated just like the example I wrote about in the military: hierarchical mentoring turned to lateral mentoring™ in a time of crisis. The mission was managed well before takeoff in a hierarchical manner. Like the military, lines of communication were hierarchical as they prepared for the mission. Once takeoff happened and a potential crisis was identified, lateral mentoring™ kicked in and Charlie consulted his lateral mentors™. They had a life-or-death problem they needed to solve. And the trust they had in lateral mentors™ allowed that to happen.

Charlie is a mentor with The Mentor Project, and he works to bring attention to the power of lateral mentoring™ by highlighting the impact having a little black book of lateral mentors™, your own version of FOC, can bring to a person. Creating a network of trusted lateral mentors™ can start in childhood like it did for Charlie, or it can start at any time in life. It is never too late.

The Start-Up Culture

lateral mentoring™ is the basis for most start-ups. The ultimate start-up was the founding of our country. Our founding fathers built this country based on lateral mentorship. Each of the founding fathers had a different area of expertise. They came together socially and over discussions, utilized the skills and talents of one another to draft the Declaration of Independence, created our Constitution, and formed the United States of America. This same way of sharing expertise to solve a problem didn't end there. It happened again very recently during the tech revolution that started in the 1970s and continues today.

Think about Steve Jobs and Steve Wozniak forming Apple. It wasn't one guy in a garage. It couldn't have been formed with just one of them. Steve and Steve mentored each other to start the company and then get it going. lateral mentoring™ in action is powerful, purposeful, and incredibly influential.

lateral mentoring™ can enhance and synergize innovation in business, technology, education, and anything else being created. This is because it creates meaningful connections among people that brings them beyond "work" or "ideas" and inspires new possibilities unimagined before. lateral mentoring™ sparks creativity and productivity because two or more individuals are working to solve a problem. One may have insights to offer, expertise, or a path to a solution that would not be possible for a single person working alone. This way of thinking brings people together not just to solve problems or to achieve a goal but to foster and nurture relationships. Think about all the times you've engaged in lateral mentorship and how good it felt and what a bonding experience it was to engage with the person you are mentoring. For me, decades later, I can remember how good it felt to help my classmate when she was in a pinch. And I can remember so many times friends have mentored me.

In fact, as I type this, I am reminded of my meeting just two days earlier with two women: Judy Berei and Debbie Lobel. They are both my lateral mentors™. Judy Berei is my husband's cousin. Our families get together at holidays, and Judy and I have a strong bond that goes beyond our family ties. Over the years, we rarely spent time talking about our work or expertise. Our conversations were generally about family and kids.

Judy holds an MBA from Yale and volunteered in the Peace Corps in Hungary. She is really smart and deeply understands the importance of giving back. About six years ago, Judy and I started talking about work. I knew she was a business leader with experiences across diverse Fortune 500 companies and start-ups. She is an industry-recognized marketing expert. When I told her about my passion for mentoring and about The Mentor Project, she immediately said, "I want to guide you to get your marketing in place." I didn't ask her; she was able to see where I could use some serious mentorship, and she asked me whether I would like to be mentored. Of course, I said yes!

Judy quickly called her good friend and colleague Debbie Lobel, who is a managing director for Edelman, a global communications firm, because she is an expert in communications and public relations. Debbie said she would like to meet, and after one meeting, she also said she would like to mentor me. It turns out Debbie has a passion for mentoring; she quickly told me about a mentoring program she was working on at her alma mater, Northwestern University. Giving back is important to Debbie, and she was on board to mentor me, along with Judy. We've met a few times on Zoom, and in each meeting, Judy and Debbie dial down enormously overwhelming problems to digestible solutions. They play off each other's expertise and give advice that I could never have come up with on my own. These two dynamic, global business leaders are my lateral mentors™, helping me to learn new aspects of business that can help move The Mentor Project to a new level.

In this case, a lateral mentor™ asked me to become my mentor. This happens more often than we realize. How many times have you noticed a friend, family member, or coworker who was fumbling around with a problem that you had the solution for? It is likely that you stepped forward as a lateral mentor™ to help them. You just didn't code it as lateral mentoring™.

It is important to acknowledge the mentoring relationship in lateral relationships. When we do, it is more likely we will step up to mentor someone or keep the engagement going. Understanding that we have helped or were helped by a lateral mentor™ makes us realize that this type of relationship is extremely valuable and makes us comfortable seeking it out and accepting it when it is offered to us.

Lateral Mentoring™ in the Workplace

Imagine being at work or in your personal life, surrounded by people who inspire you and whom you trust and look forward to spending time with.

Steve was at work with an impossible deadline looming in front of him. His boss entered his office and asked whether Steve would be able to make the deadline. This project needed to be completed, and the company's success hinged on this project being launched. Steve wasn't able to complete the job. He'd hit a wall. But there was no way he was going to tell his boss this. So, instead, he told his boss he was fine. He'd make the deadline.

His boss returned day after day but saw no progress from Steve, and he was getting anxious. He reminded Steve of the deadline and how there wasn't much time left. Steve assured him that everything was fine. But that wasn't true. Steve didn't have it. He couldn't finish it on his own. That said, he wasn't going to tell his boss this. Time was ticking, and he decided to call his buddy Steve.

Steve answered the phone at work and listened to his friend ask him whether he could help him with a work problem he was having. Steve was a wiz with all kinds of engineering and, quite honestly, was the person Steve was hanging his hopes on to help him. Steve agreed to swing by Steve's job after work. And he did. They were friends, after all, and he wanted to help him.

Steve arrived at Steve's job and took a look at the project. Steve explained where he was and what the goal was, and Steve tinkered around and started making progress right away. He stayed there and worked and worked, but no one knew he was there because it was after working hours. But he was happy to help his friend reach his goals and to help him solve the problem.

When the boss checked on Steve the next day, he noticed progress. This was exciting! That night, Steve came back. It was like Rumpelstiltskin coming in at night to spin straw into gold. Progress was made again. Steve cracked the code. In fact, night after night, he came, and the project was finished before the deadline.

Steve's boss was thrilled. The project was the video game Breakout by Atari. Al Alcorn (the grandfather of video games and inventor of Pong) was Steve Jobs's boss, and Steve's friend was Steve Wozniak.

Al Alcorn told me this story, although he saw it as Steve Jobs exploiting Steve Wozniak. However, this was years later, after the two Steves had a falling out. This wasn't exploitation. It was an example of lateral mentoring™. Steve Jobs was in a bind at work and didn't have the expertise to complete his goal—to create a video game. He didn't feel he could trust telling his boss (as often happens in hierarchical environments). Rather, he called someone he could trust. His friend Steve Wozniak had more expertise than him in the engineering required to complete the task. Steve Jobs trusted Steve Wozniak. Steve Wozniak agreed because he was meaningfully connected to Steve Jobs. They were good friends. Like any good friend, he was eager to help him. He was intrinsically motivated to do so. He didn't need pay or any kind of recognition. Steve Wozniak was being generative. He was eager to help his friend learn and to share his knowledge and expertise with him. They were equals from different workplaces, so this was a safe environment for Steve Jobs to receive mentorship from his friend.

Some may call this collaboration, but it fits all five components of mentoring: generativity, intrinsic motivation, meaningful connection, trust, and a goal. Collaboration is about working together as equals toward a common goal. This sounds similar, but mentoring is about a more experienced individual guiding and supporting a meaningfully connected, less experienced individual's growth and development without expectation of pay or recognition. And both parties must trust each other.

lateral mentoring™ focuses on learning and support between individuals who may not be at the same organizational level but have complementary skills, experiences, or perspectives. It often involves cross-functional or cross-departmental collaboration to enhance skills and knowledge. lateral mentoring™ is usually organic and not a formalized program.

Lateral Mentors™ in Meetings

On October 7, 2023, Israel was invaded by Hamas. The world was ablaze with the news of hostages and mass killings. On October 13, The Mentor Project held its usual Fridays with Fred Zoom meeting. This is a weekly meeting designed to bring mentors together each week to meet each other, learn from each other, and celebrate new happenings in the organization. For example, mentors come and share all that they like about each mentor when it is their birthday, and mentors come together to memorialize mentors who pass. Mentors unite for emotional support. Many gathered on the 13th of October to listen to mentor Avi Rabinovich and mentor Zafra Lerman talk about the crisis. Avi lives in Israel, and Zafra is a five-time Nobel Peace Prize nominee for Middle East peace, so mentors were eager to hear from them. During the compelling discussion led by Fred Klein, Peter Samuelson declared we needed to do something to promote peace in the world. Everyone on the Zoom call agreed. Peter decided he wanted to form a nonprofit to help promote peace.

Peter is an American and British film and TV producer (with at least 23 films produced) known for films such as *Revenge of the Nerds* and *Arlington Road*. He is also a prolific philanthropist. In 1982, his cousin, actress Emma Samms, founded Starlight Children's Foundation, a charity that brings entertainment and technology to children in hospitals. In 1990, he, Steven Spielberg, and General Norman Schwartzkopf founded the charity Starbright Foundation, a charity dedicated to developing media and technology-based programs to educate and empower children to cope with the medical, emotional, and social challenges of their illnesses. In 2014, he founded Aspire, a charity that teaches media for social change to undergraduate and graduate students. Most recently, he helped found ADAR, a charity to help unhoused individuals by providing portable, temporary housing.

When Peter has a passion, he finds a charity. In this case, he needed help from someone who could network and bring together a team quickly. Fred Klein, a labor law attorney and cofounder of Gotham City Networking, stepped forward and offered to help Peter get the nonprofit started. Fred knew all the right people to contact to get the nonprofit set up, to get committees set, and to gather everyone together. Peter couldn't have done this without Fred. And it never would have happened if the two weren't on a social Zoom meeting for mentors. Within days, Peter and Fred worked—Fred on the East Coast and Peter on the West Coast—to bring their respective talents together to form this newest nonprofit. The organization, with Peter as chairman and Fred as co-chair, happened because of lateral mentoring™. Peter asked for help, and because everyone in The Mentor Project meeting trusts each other, feels meaningfully connected, and is already generative and intrinsically motivated, the goal united both Peter and Fred to work together. It just required an idea, the goal, and the ask.

Many innovative and fulfilled people are engaged in lateral mentoring™ but don't have a label for it, nor do they realize how powerful it is. It is an intuitive form of mentoring that is generally trust-driven, with an immediate problem that needs to be solved. We call on someone we trust to guide us, help us solve a problem, or give us advice, just as a hierarchical mentor would, but in the case of the lateral mentor™, it isn't formal, often not labeled, and therefore, often not acknowledged. Imagine all of the times you've asked for help or guidance from someone. Now, think of how often you've acknowledged that as mentorship. By simply acknowledging lateral mentorship, we will likely engage in it more often. We will see the value of it and crave more and more of it!

Peer Mentoring

Hierarchical mentoring, peer mentoring, and lateral mentoring™ share similarities as they all involve learning and support between individuals and all share the five key components of mentoring. Where they differ is in their focus and context.

Peer mentoring focuses on mutual learning and support between peers who may be at the same level within an organization, academic program, or community. It's about sharing knowledge, experiences, and insights to help each other grow. Most often, we see peer mentoring in schools and youth, with peers mentoring other peers. Peer mentoring is usually acknowledged and organized rather than developed organically. Peer mentors are especially likely to share information, provide feedback on career strategizing, and offer emotional support (Eby et al. 2015). In addition, peer mentoring relationships are marked by greater mutuality and similar amounts of psychosocial support but less instrumental support than hierarchical mentoring relationships. Common examples of peer mentoring are school peer mentoring programs where a student mentors a fellow student who is struggling in a particular subject of learning. It can also be seen with colleagues with similar job roles supporting each other. Peer mentoring has many components of lateral mentoring™, but the main difference is that lateral mentoring™ is organic in nature, and peer mentoring is often a set program.

Peer Mentoring in the Workplace

In academic medicine, the higher you get, the harder is to find mentors, especially for women. Dr. Miriam Bredella (who you will learn more about in Chapter 7) has worked in academic hospital settings and has found that it is very difficult for a woman who is a full professor to find a mentor in the hierarchical work setting. Dr. Bredella started a peer mentoring group to help support women academics in Massachusetts General Hospital (MGH), a Harvard hospital. The group met every other week. This group was so cohesive and became so meaningfully connected that Miriam is still in touch with them even though she's moved on to another hospital (in another state). The women from the peer mentoring group still contact her, and they still support each other and have branched out beyond mentoring and have started sponsoring each other by nominating each other for awards.

The group started with the women mentoring each other by guiding each other with a goal of career advancement. The women would find out what experience and area of expertise each of the others had and would help answer career questions so they could advance by joining boards or committees. This was so successful and the women were so generative with their mentoring that they expanded the program for associate and assistant professors. They were especially successful with mid career academics because this is when most people in this group think they have everything they need to advance in their careers but are also the most unhappy, because although they've accomplished a great deal, no one really acknowledges their success and they go unnoticed. The peer mentoring group helped them to get eyes on them and to focus on their accomplishments to get them to move up the ranks. The guidance from peers was helpful because they could open up and connect with others who were in the same "boat."

The group was semiformal and had an administrator who helped to coordinate times when everyone could meet as a group. Sometimes they had a topic to discuss, but it was often peers helping each other with issues that kept them up at night—whether work or personal. This semi-structure led to deeper connections and even moving some of the gatherings to people's homes. The connections became meaningful and trusted. Navigating the workplace wasn't a feat to accomplish alone. There were peer mentors there to help and guide, which was powerful both emotionally and professionally.

Peer Mentoring vs. Lateral Mentoring™

- **Peer mentoring** focuses on personal and professional development, skill enhancement, and mutual support within a peer group. The goals are often aligned with shared experiences and common challenges.

- **Lateral mentoring™** focuses on leveraging diverse perspectives, skills, and experiences to foster innovation, problem-solving, and collaboration across different areas or departments within an organization.
- **Peer mentoring** can be more informal and organic, developing naturally within peer groups or communities. It may not have a designated mentorship structure or program.
- **Lateral mentoring™** can be more structured, especially in organizational settings, where specific mentoring programs or initiatives encourage cross-functional collaboration and knowledge sharing.

Although both peer mentoring and lateral mentoring™ involve learning and support among individuals with similar experiences or complementary skills, they differ in their focus (mutual support vs. cross-functional collaboration), hierarchy (similar vs. different levels), purpose (personal/professional development vs. innovation/collaboration), and structure (informal vs. structured).

Mentoring is available in every aspect of our lives. We are able to be guided by a person more senior than us, in a hierarchical manner, or by a trusted friend or peer. We should be accessing all forms of mentorship whenever possible. We gain when we mentor and we gain when we are mentored. In the case of mentoring, there isn't ever too much of a good thing. We can never get or give too much mentoring! In the next chapter, you will find examples of mentors engaging in a variety of styles and in personal and professional settings.

6 Mentors in Our Lives

So many people tell me they don't mentor. But they do! According to the National Center for Education Statistics, there were 3.5 million full- and part-time traditional public school teachers in the 2020–2021 school year. They are one of the strongest sets of mentors we have, shaping our children and young adults. There are also private school teachers, university professors, and trade school teachers.

The Teacher

Susan Crook was born in 1949 and raised in Des Moines, Iowa. She was a smart girl who, from the time she turned five and started school, knew she wanted to teach. She never wavered and considers herself very lucky to have chosen a field that exceeded her expectations. She finished high school, went straight to college, and started teaching first grade in 1971.

Sue taught for 40 years. The job she had dreamed about for nearly 20 years began as a nightmare. She was overwhelmed and felt entirely unprepared when faced with a classroom full of six-year-olds. Fortunately, Grace Green, a seasoned teacher in the classroom next to hers, noticed Sue needed some guidance. She took Sue under her wing and provided mentorship over the course of the year. As Sue describes it, this turned her first year from frightening to "an awesome experience." Grace and Sue remained close, with Grace serving as her mentor for many years. They fell out of touch for several years when they no longer taught in the same school. It was when Sue found out Grace's granddaughter was a student in her class that they reconnected. Sue was thrilled to see her original mentor at school conferences and Grandparents Day. She felt great pride knowing Grace felt confident in Sue's ability to teach her granddaughter.

When Sue turned 50, No Child Left Behind, an act of Congress (2001–2002) that mandated a standards-based education reform was implemented in Iowa schools. Sue was one of the ground-level teachers selected to train mentors in the program. She was a "mentor of mentors." For 10 years, she taught many teachers how to mentor other teachers. She loved the experience and felt fulfilled as she passed on her skills to newer teachers. Following this, the school she had been teaching in for 20 years asked her to mentor first-year teachers. This one-on-one mentoring was similar to what Sue received from Grace many years ago. She found it especially meaningful because she was not only preparing these teachers for their future with regard to obtaining their required certifications, but she also provided them with emotional support. Like Grace did for her, she listened to them and didn't offer unsolicited advice. Rather, she waited for them to come to her when they felt they needed help.

This technique was so successful that many teachers who weren't even her assigned mentees came to her home on weekends to learn from her. She describes her joy in working with the young teachers as "fulfilling." She felt a kinship with these women that went beyond classroom mentorship. She became close with many of them, and they remain friends today, decades later.

At 65, Sue's close friendships include her mentees, past and present. These mentees and their children and grandchildren became extended family, and although she didn't have children of her own, her family became large and extended, just as if she had.

These relationships continue to be incredibly meaningful to her. Sue is satisfied that she was a good mentor and that she leaves a legacy of good teachers who are continuing the work she has valued since she started school at age five.

After writing this, I posted it on Sue Crook's Facebook timeline, and it exploded. The number of comments from her former mentees was overwhelming. One comment was particularly moving. A former student from about two decades earlier wrote to Sue telling her how lucky she was to have her as a teacher for three years in elementary school. She was an abused child by her stepfather, whose mom worked three jobs to support all of them. Sue wasn't aware of what was happening in her home after school. This student had so many issues outside of school that affected her ability to perform in the classroom. Sue noticed her, was patient, talked with her, and even had her move her desk right next to Sue's as she taught class. She made her feel special and important. On many occasions, the student and her mother would walk over to Sue's house unannounced for visits. Sue always invited them in to spend time with her. Before Sue, the student said school was just an escape from home. But, after three years of having Sue as a teacher, she started to appreciate reading poetry and memorizing the presidents in order. She found she was good at reading and really good at memorizing. She began to excel. Her low self-esteem faded, and she continued to excel in school after leaving Sue's classroom. She became the first in her family to graduate high school and the first to graduate college. She became a registered nurse and credited Sue with profoundly influencing her life through the guidance and mentorship Sue gave her when she was young. It wasn't until she saw the Facebook post that she let her feelings flow, finally telling her mentor from many years ago just how much her life had transformed because of her mentoring.

She ended her post by saying Sue was an inspiration to her and she will always hold a special place in her heart for Sue.

Sue couldn't believe the impact she had on this former student or on the lives of all the people who came forward to tell stories of how her mentorship improved their lives. Sue wrote: "I honestly had no idea what she was going through. I LOVED teaching, and those first few years (I was pretty green), allowed me to really enjoy interactions with the kids. I lived in the neighborhood and lots of the kids stopped in to see me. I loved that too. I miss teaching because I felt clear down inside that I was quietly changing little lives. I never needed accolades (you don't really get that from adults in teaching often anyway), but the bright smiles and shining eyes of those children were enough to fill me up and keep me going. I also didn't realize until after retiring, that teaching fulfilled me. I don't get the warmth as a retired person that I felt when I could make a difference in a life. However, I know that my current energy level would not allow for me to continue teaching if I wanted to. It's a compromise you have to make when you retire."

Sue's legacy continues in each of the former students and colleagues she mentored over the years. Many people believe you need to bear children in order to leave a legacy and fear that if they do not have children, they cannot leave a legacy. Sue's story shows that mentorship can lead to a legacy by connecting to individuals at a deep level. You don't need a biological connection.

Sue's motivation was intrinsic. She met with fellow faculty, student teachers, students, and families outside of school on her own time. Sue wasn't mentoring for the money. Yet, she felt fulfilled for 40 years and felt passionate about her work. Sue is not unique. The number of mentees teachers have is enormous, and their impact goes well beyond their job trajectory. It's not all about academics. Teachers mentor emotional support and model behavior to strive for. And that is at least as important.

The Professor

A professor's duties encompass far more than classroom lectures and academic advisement; they often include the invaluable act of mentoring students. However, the concept of mentoring within academia can be puzzling given that professors are paid for their instructional roles. This juxtaposition raises the question: How can extrinsically motivated interactions truly be considered mentoring? Especially when one of the quintessential elements of mentorship is intrinsic motivation.

Most people don't realize that professors mentor and work with their students outside the classroom and during off hours all the time. They mentor off the clock, just like Sue Crook did when she was meeting with her students outside of school hours. The lines are blurred a bit, and the intrinsic motivation is able to take over even while the "clock is ticking" during work hours.

Professor Neil Comins is an example. He teaches in the Department of Physics and Astronomy at the University of Maine. Neil has written over 20 books, one of which is *What if the Moon Didn't Exist?*, which became the basis of a television show in Japan and resulted in a cartoon character of Neil that still exists today. He presents his work around the globe, is an international speaker, and has had 29 grants funded. Dr. Comins is also a prolific mentor at his university and with The Mentor Project.

Dr. Comins' own journey is a testament to the transformative power of mentorship. Neil had a really tough childhood. He was incredibly smart and oozed talent and curiosity in areas most of us would never even know existed, but his parents were abusive and belittled him, so he didn't have a chance to understand how smart he was or the options he had for his future. Neil had low self-esteem, which you'd never know now. He's flown airplanes in places most people never dream of, is a skydiver, a ham radio operator, author, and is a loving father and husband. Friends of his joke that there isn't anything Neil hasn't done.

When I asked Neil to tell me about his mentees, he told me he needed to start by telling me about his mentor, because he would not be a mentor today if it were not for the person who mentored him. Professor Charles Misner was a physicist specializing in general relativity and cosmology, coauthor of *Gravitation*, a widely adopted textbook on the general theory of relativity, and Neil's mentor at the University of Maryland in College Park in the mid-1970s. Neil remained close to Professor Misner for more than 50 years until he passed away in 2023 at the age of 91. He had a profound impact on Neil's life.

Neil was a graduate student tasked with grading papers for professors, and one assignment was to grade papers for Professor Misner's General Relativity course. Neil found the subject matter in the papers he was grading interesting and would stop to ask Professor Misner questions as they arose. The conversations became more personal, and one day Neil told the professor he was an amateur radio operator (then known as a ham radio operator). A ham radio isn't like the kind of radio you listen to in the car for news, sports, and music. It uses radio frequency spectrum for noncommercial message exchanges between individuals, wireless experimentation, emergency communication, and private recreation. Living the grad student life didn't afford Neil the space for the necessary equipment to house his ham radio station. When Professor Misner learned Neil couldn't operate his ham radio because he needed a place to house the radio station, he invited Neil to set up his radio station at his house. This was the beginning of their mentoring relationship. Every week Neil went to Charlie's house. He didn't just use the ham radio—he became a part of Charlie's family. They developed a friendship, which continued until the day Charlie died. Neil became particularly close with one of Charlie's children, and this relationship became part of a multipronged experience. Neil learned science, graded Charlie's papers, and interacted with his family. He essentially became a member of the family.

Professor Misner probably didn't realize it, but Neil needed a positive father figure. Neil's academic gifts needed to be nurtured, and he needed to find a way to balance work and relationships. Professor Misner became that figure for him and mentored him by providing emotional support and educational guidance that helped him overcome his childhood challenges. Neil moved beyond seeing him as just his professor and saw him as a mentor who transformed his life. Charlie also benefited. He had a "son" who loved the work he did and was eager to learn from him any chance he got. He was rewarded by Neil's enthusiasm, and their relationship flourished well beyond work.

When Neil decided to leave the University of Maryland, Charlie guided him and helped him get a graduate position at the University College in Cardiff, Wales. Charlie was much more than a professor. He was a meaningful connection. He was a mentor in the best sense of the word.

Now it has come full circle as Neil is paying it forward. Neil is a professor at the University of Maine, and he mentors students. He will tell anyone who asks that he enjoys mentoring students because of his positive experience with his mentor, Charlie. One mentoring relationship that stands out for Neil is a student named Graham Van Goffrier, who is so bright and talented he could have gone to Harvard. Still, he was raised near the University of Maine by a single mom, and it was just easier for him to attend the University of Maine. Graham reminded Neil of himself when he was Graham's age.

Graham took one of Neil's classes and enjoyed it so much that he took another. Neil noticed Graham's enthusiasm for the subject matter, which led him into areas he wouldn't have been able to explore otherwise. These included general relativity and the background mathematics needed to understand it. All of this interaction was within Neil's normal work hours, but it started changing because Graham understood everything Neil presented to him, which didn't happen often with other students. They started having more conversations, much like Neil and Charlie did, and Neil found himself feeling like a father figure to Graham. The two formed a deep and meaningful connection, with Neil guiding and supplying new concepts to Graham, who was thirsty to learn and have a direction for his future. The similarities between Neil and Charlie's relationship and Neil and Graham's were uncanny.

Graham and Neil's mentoring relationship was a two-way street. Neil saw enormous potential in Graham and would introduce new concepts to him and guide him when he found new opportunities for him. Graham would seek out Neil when he needed more information and when he needed guidance to help him move forward. Their mentoring relationship culminated in Neil's recommendation of Graham for a master's program at Cambridge University in England. Graham got in and then followed that with a PhD at University College London. Even with the distance, Neil and Graham are close like Neil and Charlie. The key to both Neil and Charlie as mentors is that much of their mentoring happened outside official working hours. Even though they connected during the work/school day, their relationship flourished outside the classroom and during office hours as well. They moved beyond student/professor and became mentor/mentee and friends. They are still close today, and Neil feels just as excited about Graham's accomplishments as he does his own sons'.

The crux of effective mentoring lies in its ability to foster genuine connections that transcend formal boundaries. In the case of Sue Crook, an elementary school teacher, and Neil Comins, a university professor, mentorship flourished through authentic relationships that facilitated mutual growth and support. In the realm of education, mentorship emerges as a cornerstone of professional development, forging enduring connections that enrich both mentors and mentees alike.

Grandparents

The Grandpa

My first mentor was my grandfather, Charles S. Crook, II, a decorated captain in the US Army in World War II, who is now buried in Arlington Cemetery.

As soon as I turned five, my grandfather made it a tradition to pick me up in his big 1970s Cadillac convertible to run errands with him in downtown Des Moines, Iowa. He was a six-foot-tall man with a booming voice and a swagger that let you know he wasn't anybody's fool. He wasn't exactly warm and fuzzy, but he and I understood one another and enjoyed our trips out together each week.

Along the ride across and through town, as we drove by people on the streets, he told me all about them (I don't know if any of it was true, but as a five-year-old, I ate it all up like candy). He'd say, "You see that man over on the right? The one walking fast? His wife chewed him out five minutes ago for forgetting to bring home the dry cleaning. He's mad as hell right now at her and walking around to cool off. She's one nasty lady." A bit later, we'd pass another person sitting on a bench. "See Mary over there on the bench? She raised two girls. They went to college, and Mary made sure it happened for them. Her husband ran out on them when they were young. She has a hard life." He never ran out of stories about the people we'd pass. These conversations made me see each person I ever passed on the street as a real person from then on. Someone with a story. Someone who had the power to make a difference, whether good or bad, in the lives of others.

Grandpa was a man who followed his beliefs to the end—and taught me at an early age to follow my convictions regardless of what others think. I don't say this lightly. My white grandfather, who moved from Baltimore, Maryland, to live with my grandmother to raise six kids in Iowa after the war, found discrimination against minorities (racial and religious) to be intolerable. By the time he started taking me around town on his errands, he was entrenched in the civil rights movement and, during this time, was the president of the Des Moines, Iowa, chapter of the NAACP.

Each week, we stopped for breakfast at the local pancake shop (named Sambo's—of all names). I noticed that people wouldn't sit next to us. Many people said rude things to him and gave me dirty looks as we ate our pancakes. On one occasion (our last), the waitress watered down our orange juice, and when Grandpa complained, the manager came to our table and actually repoured a glass for my grandpa. He poured the orange juice into the glass, stopped halfway, took a water pitcher, dispensed the water right into the same glass as the orange juice, and filled it up to the top. Then he just turned and walked away.

During all our time each week running Grandpa's errands (going to the post office, stopping in at his office, or going to the grocery store and having a pancake breakfast), he never told me anything about his involvement in the civil rights movement. But what I took in during our weekly time together was that he didn't care that the rude people didn't like him. For a while, I didn't like this about him. I felt uncomfortable with waitresses giving dirty looks and patrons sitting far away from us and mumbling comments about Grandpa under their breath as they passed us. I didn't want to go out with him on his errands for a few months. I'd beg my mom to let me stay home.

The peak of embarrassment was when his neighbors from his nice middle-class neighborhood across the street from the golf course talked about him at the park, and kids talked about him in school. I found myself squirming when people asked if he was my grandpa. They said he was "integrating" the neighborhood and the church. I had no idea what the word "integrating" was, and I knew enough to realize it wasn't a popular concept. I wrestled with knowing he cared about people but knowing that he wasn't doing something people liked. Over time, I saw that he was helping people. He also said that he didn't let those who didn't like him stop him from pursuing his beliefs. Time allowed me to integrate my feelings and to understand that sometimes we do the right thing even when we know the road to making change isn't easy. His guidance over the years showed me that if we want to change something, we have to speak and act. Hoping, wishing, and complaining won't work. We need to see the world outside ourselves and realize we, as individuals, are just a part of the big picture.

My grandpa is long gone, but I still hear his voice on my shoulder telling me there is a story in every person. Every person matters. He is probably one of the reasons why I became a psychologist (and married one). He is probably one of the reasons I've advocated for the aging for two decades. He passed the torch to me, and I will pass the torch to my children.

The Nana

Nana Brendolyn is the mother of a friend I worked with years ago. She and I met in person for the first time on the day of her daughter's husband Odell's memorial service. Odell's death was untimely and tragic. Odell, his wife, and their toddler moved to New York City so Odell could finish his oral surgery training. He'd already completed his doctorate in dentistry but wanted to get an additional specialization in oral surgery. Odell's training was in New York, and they needed to move there from Atlanta. There was a complicating factor in their move. Odell learned he had cancer while in his program. His wife was working, and Odell was in school and training, and they were both trying to manage his cancer treatment. To say they were busy and overwhelmed would be an understatement. They needed to have their young son stay in Atlanta with Nana Brendolyn to be cared for. It was expected to be temporary.

Just until his training ended.

Brendolyn made life easier for everyone and swooped in to help with her grandson. He was just a toddler, but Brendolyn had goals for this young child. She wanted to make sure he grew up with values and morals and manners. The same she grew up with and the same she passed on to her children. This was very important to her, and a legacy she wanted to leave behind. So, in addition to being his nana, she became Odell Jr.'s mentor.

After Odell's passing, his wife moved back to Atlanta; she got a job, and Brendolyn continued to help her daughter raise her son. When I asked Brendolyn about grandparenting and how she felt about it, she said she always took her role very seriously. Mentoring was a big part of her role as a grandparent. She taught her grandson how to be honest and taught him morals and good values. She lived an honest, moral life, modeling for him what she expected of him. They had a wonderful bond. She always told the truth so he would learn that it is best to be truthful. Her goal was to help guide him to be a good person and a good adult one day. As Odell got older, she'd tell him to always be honest with her and to be honest with his mother because they were always going to be the people to go to bat for him if something didn't go right.

Brendolyn was profoundly proud of her grandson. She never got called to the school for a problem. In church, everyone spoke well of him. She worked with him every day after school, and she will tell everyone that she tries not to brag about him, but she is grateful that he turned out the way he has.

She has every right to feel great. I met her grandson when he was just a baby. He attended our wedding with his parents. Roughly 14 years later, he then came with his mom and Nana to visit my family at our house in New York. He was remarkably well-mannered, smart, and kind. He reminded me of his father. Brendolyn was, of course, proud. She was able to see the values, morals, and kindness in her grandson. Her mentoring goals had been met with success. Her legacy was her grandson, and it was the legacy she wanted when he was just a baby.

Brendolyn's mentoring of her grandson was crucial to her. Her grandson became the smart, well-mannered, kind adult she hoped he would be. It wasn't an accident. She had a goal to raise him with values, morals, and kindness. And it worked. His respect and love for her and kindness to others were clear as he was setting off on his adult journey.

Mentoring Full Circle

Rebecca "Becky" Bace was a pioneer in and one of the most influential leaders of cybersecurity and information security. She was named one of the top five women in security by *Information Security Magazine* in 1993. She received the Distinguished Leadership Award for her work at the National Security Agency. She was also an entrepreneur and an author. Becky was brilliant and talented, but these accomplishments didn't come easily, and they didn't come without the help and guidance of many mentors along the way. As she wound down her career, she found herself guiding and helping others, just as others had done for her.

Here is Becky's story:

Becky started life with two strikes against her. She was born with epilepsy, and she was one of seven children, without significant means in the Deep South, to an Alabama long haul trucker and a Japanese immigrant. Her appearance presented some confusion for those she encountered growing up. There were no other families like hers where she lived, and most people who met her expected her to speak "pigeon English" rather than her native Alabama drawl. Becky's father was away a lot of the time, and her mom was understandably overwhelmed raising seven children on her own in a new country, without her family for support. One might think a family with seven children living on a trucker's salary would spell doom for Becky's chances to make a significant mark on the world. Think again.

Becky's first mentor was a close family friend as well as the high school librarian, BerthaNel Allen. Becky was good friends with BerthaNel's daughter and spent a lot of time with the Allen family. BerthaNel could tell Becky's mom was overwhelmed, but she also noticed Becky's intelligence and academic potential. BerthaNel stepped in, became a second mother to Becky, and became her first guide to a successful future. BerthaNel's help was consistent and concrete. Just what a young person needs. In eighth and ninth grade, BerthaNel helped Becky make connections to get her first job as a librarian assistant in the city library. She taught Becky how to become competitive in high school coursework so she could get scholarships for college and helped her fill out those college and scholarship applications. Through BerthaNel's guidance, Becky applied for and received an early entry scholarship for a summer at Sanford University in Alabama and was awarded two scholarships. These scholarships allowed her to attend college—University of Alabama at Birmingham—when she financially would not have been able to otherwise. At the time she was preparing to attend college, neurologists treating Becky for her epilepsy suggested she sign up for disability rather than attend. Becky didn't even consider this as an option. BerthaNel's guidance, support, and belief in her helped her to see that she could, indeed, attend college.

In late 1988, Becky started working at the National Computer Security Center (NCSC, which was chartered as part of the National Security Agency [NSA] expressly to deal with computer security issues for the US Department of Defense and the intelligence community). There, she met Jim Anderson, a mentor who laid the groundwork for modern computer security and who also worked in computer security at NSA. As stated by Becky, "Jim Anderson was one of the leaders of the computer security community (as well as a pioneer in computing). I was in a position where I had a friend/colleague/mentor relationship with him that seriously influenced my life path. Though my official supervisors at NCSC/NSA all knew and respected Jim (who advised most of their supervisors and directors), our relationship was not one of supervisor-employee. He did a lot of things for me. He answered my questions about the needs that first initiated the research that resulted in his intrusion detection paper. The conversation continued, and he made himself available to me for opinions as I considered how best to bring the research to useful form given the resources I had available. Over time, he made introductions, brought me and the program to the attention of folks above me who were in a position to help, and, as the community of researchers and other stakeholders grew, pitched in as a member of that community—people still tell me to this day how much that access influenced their careers." Jim gave Becky the start her career needed just when she needed it.

Another example of Jim's mentorship, as stated by Becky: "The year was 1999, and I was researching my first book (on intrusion detection) and in a bit of a panic. I had a running email conversation with Jim, and I told him that I wanted to be unusually rigorous in outlining the history of audit mechanisms (that were the main source of information used by early intrusion detection systems) in computer systems. He told me a wonderful story of how a discussion of audit trails with a neighbor of his—who was the lead engineer for the Bell telephone system, tasked with designing an audit system for Bell's first business computer system—led to the intrusion detection work. He also looked back in the notes he'd taken at the time and gave me a rough pointer to an article his neighbor had written in the mid-1960s about the design of that system. I was able to go to the local UC campus library, find the article in question, and include it in the book, which was warmly received." Jim was a constant source of help and guidance when Becky needed him. She could trust him, and his help was always valued. Once again, an important project (in this case, her book) was improved because of his knowledge and guidance.

Another mentor to Becky during her time with NSA was Bob Abbot, a peer who became her lateral mentor™. As Becky recalls, "He was the water walker for the commercial side of security. He was a computing pioneer with a career that started in the early 1950s when he joined Lawrence Livermore National Laboratory as a computer scientist. I met Bob in the early 1990s, when I was pulling together a set of community discussion workshops and wanted a historical view of commercial computer audit process— one study he had done in the mid-1970s was considered seminal to the area, so when I found one of my researchers knew him, I was thrilled to have a chance to meet him and furthermore have him join us for the workshop. Later, he served as consultant/advisor for some of my portfolio firms, where he advised them on how best to approach major corporate clients. He told me, shortly before he died, that this opportunity to reenter the security world was like being given another life. I felt that Bob not only served as a mentor, but also served an additional function as someone I could count on as a trust anchor and advocate. If he thought I was making a mistake, he would let me know about it; it was understood that I returned the favor."

A thread that runs through the mentoring as described by Becky is trust. A mentor must be someone a mentee can trust for the relationship to work. Without trust, a mentee will constantly question whether or not to take their mentor's advice, and will question whether or not the help being offered is useful. Trust allows us to accept the guidance, connections, and information the mentor is offering.

Jim Anderson continued to mentor Becky even after she left the NSA and went to Silicon Valley in the middle of the dot-com boom. He used his connections to get her a room and to become connected in the area. Becky entered a new field: venture consulting. Peter Meekin stepped in as her next mentor, and together they built one of the largest portfolios in Silicon Valley. As stated by Becky, "Peter and I have a different relationship from that I had with Jim and Bob. Peter is brilliant as well, but far more reserved. He is generous but also made a point of including me in the investment process, making a point to share background on how and why decisions were being made. He was responsible for overseeing the operations of firms in which we'd made investments, and I loved being able to discuss how he did this in an area that was a bit alien to me. He made a point of fielding all sorts of questions from me in ways that felt like an interaction with a favorite professor or consultant—he remains a far better VC and corporate exec than I'll ever be, but he shared so much of his process with me in ways that built out my skill set in valuable ways." Becky is humble. She became one of the most influential people in Internet security and mentored many start-ups.

Becky had a wild, long ride with the NSA, Silicon Valley, and venture consulting, and then came full circle. She found herself back where she started. She went back to Alabama and took a job with a part-time appointment at a university. At this stage of her life, she became the mentor. Her last mentee was CEO Jeehay Yun of Red Shred in Maryland. "Jeehye asserts that my current mentoring duty with her is 'talking her off the ledge on bad days.' Having common cultural exposure works well (they both had Asian immigrant mothers). Here, as I understand all too well how we were raised to be a wee bit critical of ourselves. A lot of what I do is a mix of connection-making, sanity checking, and comforting/reminding Jeehye to cut herself some slack, at times with scheduled meetings for lunch or visits to the local Asian bakery as reinforcement. I do use a lot of the mentoring skills I've seen in action, but as much of my approach to interacting with Jeehye comes from my interaction with my sisters. I think that having traveled the path before (as entrepreneur, geek girl, mother, Asian daughter) buys me credibility as a mentor in ways that are likely a bit different from that I might have had were I male (as were a fair number of my mentors)."

Becky's life was changed by the mentors in her life. They offered trust, guidance, support, knowledge, and a belief in her abilities. Becky could have lived a life collecting disability, never leaving the town where she was raised. Instead, she became a pioneer in computer security and one of the top five most influential women in the field. Becky stated that her first mentor, BerthaNel, was always delighted when something good happened for her, up until she died. BerthaNel opened the door for Becky and changed one young girl's life forever.

It then became Becky's turn to change the lives of others she mentored. Becky passed away in 2017, but her mentees carry her wisdom, and they are her legacy. Multiple awards have been established in her memory, including the Scholarships for Women Studying Information Security (SWSIS) and the Rebecca Bace Pioneer Award for Defensive Security. The mentoring circle continues.

The Mentor Project

Mentorship has played a crucial role in the personal and professional growth of mentee Lily Osman. For Lily, the importance of having a mentor, who believes in her and her work, providing her with valuable insights and guidance, is invaluable. Mentorship has had an enormous impact on her dreams and goals. She reached heights she didn't think she would, in part because her mentors expressed enthusiasm for tapping into Lily's talents, guiding her to new levels, and showcasing her accomplishments. She has benefited from the relationship with her mentor, and they continue to meet weekly, more than two years after their initial meeting. Her emotional growth has been as successful as her tangible accomplishments.

Lily Osman's journey with her mentors in The Mentor Project is not just a story of professional growth but also one of personal transformation and empowerment. Her mentors have been pivotal in shaping her path as a designer, innovator, and entrepreneur, guiding her through the intricate process of patenting her ideas, mentoring her in product design, and nurturing her emotional development.

It all began with an experience during Lily's time in culinary school, where she recognized the discomfort women faced with traditional knife holds. Most people just let it go, but she thought she could do something about it. This idea led her to The Mentor Project, to seek mentorship from people whose extensive experience and successful track record with patents made for a perfect guide for Lily's entrepreneurial aspirations.

When Lily entered culinary school, she just thought she was really good at cooking. She went in confident about her skills, and then, on the very first day of school, she found out she wasn't holding her knife properly. When she figured out the correct way to hold the knife, it wasn't comfortable. A female chef in her first level of cooking school told Lily, "Knives aren't made for us," meaning women. Lily learned that knives are designed for men. She was told she would have to work harder to make up for this. Her hands were smaller than a man's and the grip and feel of the knives wasn't optimal for her. Lily thought, "This can't be the case." So she started looking into professional knives and found out that the instructor was right. This sent Lily into motion. She started drawing ideas that would make the knife more comfortable for a woman's hand. But these were only dreams at this point, and she put her drawings and ideas aside.

When Lily entered her master's program, she took a food entrepreneurship course, and she pitched her knife idea to her class and its professor. They encouraged her to pursue her idea. But she still didn't know how to go about taking the next steps. It turned out her dad found out about The Mentor Project, and he told Lily about it. She wasn't keen on trying something he suggested because she wanted to figure it out on her own, but she reached out anyway.

She was matched with the person who became her primary mentor, shortly thereafter. Her mentor's encouragement was not just a push in the right direction; it was a catalyst that ignited Lily's journey. Under this mentorship, she not only learned the technicalities of patenting but also gained the confidence to form her own company and bring her product designs to life. Their weekly brainstorming sessions over two years became more than just discussions about patents; they were moments of inspiration, guidance, and unwavering support.

Their first meeting set the tone. As Lily recalled, she had never talked to someone who had a successful company on the scale of the mentors who are part of The Mentor Project. Many are serial entrepreneurs and innovators. While Lily believed in herself, she couldn't say enough about how mentors with such impressive résumés, believing in her, really kick-started her desire to launch a company and innovate new kitchenware. Her dreams now had the potential to become a reality. After working with a mentor for only one week, she didn't feel alone. This was tremendously helpful to her, knowing she had an emotional sounding board and a safety net. A mentor was going to lead her in the right direction and guide her away from mistakes she might be drawn to make as a new entrepreneur. She ran her ideas by mentors, and they would insert their ideas, which helped to build her ideas to bigger, better-functioning ideas. For example, she played with magnets on the floor to see how they might be used with her knives.

She did this, and now the magnet is a huge part of the knife pattern and a huge part of the idea. As Lily says, "Just having access to this very extensive mind and allowing me to kind of remain expansive instead of getting bogged down made all the difference." She wasn't getting caught up in the weeds. She was thinking more broadly than ever before.

Then the Innovation Lab at The Mentor Project was launched, and a group of mentors and mentees started meeting each week. At this point, she is fine-tuning the work, and Lily and a mentor talk every week on Zoom. She considers them friends now. The mentors may be decades apart in age, but they enjoy meeting and talking every week, even if it isn't about Lily's project or the book. They've gone way beyond Lily's original idea.

For Lily, her mentor is more than a mentor; he's a mentor who believes in her vision and champions her success. She fondly describes him as a "crazy uncle" who is passionate about seeing her thrive, and she sees herself as a part of his legacy, a testament to his mentorship and guidance.

The mentorship has not only helped Lily navigate the complexities of entrepreneurship but has also instilled in her the values of embracing her identity as a creative and gifted entrepreneur, being vocal about her ideas, and adapting to challenges with resilience. Through mentorship, Lily has found her passion, achieved her goals, and emerged as a successful entrepreneur and innovator, all while acknowledging the profound impact of mentorship on her journey of growth and self-discovery—and feeling really good about herself.

The mentorship Lily receives with The Mentor Project helps her see herself and the world in a new light, fostering growth and collaboration with others. She is seeking success but, as all good mentors know, success is subjective. Support from mentors can help mentees reach their goals; it can also help mitigate the inevitable failures. They are all part of the process, part of the journey. Lily and her primary mentor, Bob, are enjoying that journey as they navigate it together.

Mentors provided more than half a million dollars' worth of mentoring during the last calendar year. Between the Innovation Lab and individual mentoring hours, Lily worked together for roughly four hours every week that year. Everyone involved feels valued by this relationship, which is an emotional gift just as valuable as monetary exchange. It is a win-win.

Lily Osman's journey with mentorship has not only transformed her professional life but also ignited her passion to pay it forward by mentoring young entrepreneurs in the Innovation Lab. Inspired by her own experiences, Lily is driven to inspire newcomers to pursue their passions boldly, free from the fear of making mistakes. Exactly as she learned to do.

Having navigated self-doubt and insecurities herself, Lily understands the transformative power of emotional support and guidance from a mentor. Her mentor's encouragement and belief in her abilities pushed her to enter her design into a prestigious award competition. The result? A resounding victory as she clinched an International Design Award, outshining 100,000 other applicants from 80 countries. Talk about validation.

This success wasn't just about winning an award; it was about opening doors to possibilities Lily hadn't imagined she could reach before. It fueled her determination to accomplish even more and served as a testament to the impact of mentorship on her journey.

Now, as she reflects on her achievements, Lily recognizes the importance of having someone to turn to for guidance, advice, and the courage to face challenges head-on. She believes that acknowledging and celebrating accomplishments are crucial steps in personal growth and plans to leverage her experiences to mentor others effectively.

For Lily, mentoring isn't just about sharing knowledge; it's about providing unwavering support, helping others overcome fears, and guiding them through obstacles on their path to innovation and success. Her dedication to serving as a mentor stems from a deep understanding of how powerful mentorship can be in transforming dreams into reality.

Mentoring is a transformative journey that transcends the boundaries of traditional education. It delves into emotional realms, forging deep connections between mentors and mentees as they embark on shared dreams and aspirations. In this synergistic relationship, the mentor's goals intertwine with the mentee's, creating a bond that goes beyond mere guidance—it becomes a shared mission to the benefit of both parties.

Measuring the impact of mentoring isn't just about tangible outcomes; it's about the profound emotional transformations that are the result of good mentoring. The sense of trust, security, usefulness, relevance, and validation that mentors and mentees experience are enduring emotional successes that shape their paths long after the mentoring relationship ends.

Whereas tangible success can be more easily quantified than emotional impact, the latter is at least as important. The gratification and fulfillment mentoring provides is immeasurable yet hugely significant. It fosters an inner sense of purpose, belonging, and personal growth that extends far beyond professional achievements. Ultimately, successful mentor-mentee relationships epitomize the essence of human connection and the profound influence of guidance, support, and understanding on our journeys to fulfillment and success.

Mentors and mentees come in all shapes and sizes, spanning various ages and professions. They might be the familiar faces we encounter daily, the ones who quietly shape our lives. Mentors, like seasoned navigators, guide us through uncharted waters, imparting their wisdom and values. As mentees, we carry their legacy forward, weaving their teachings into our own narratives. The mentor-mentee relationship resembles a wheel, perpetually turning and propelling us forward. While we recognize how mentors enhance our personal lives, their impact extends to our professional realms as well. In workplaces, mentorship becomes a compass, steering us toward growth, resilience, and collaboration. The next chapter delves into workplace mentorship, exploring how it transforms interactions and fosters collective progress.

7 Mentoring in the Workplace

Mentoring in the workplace is complex, even when it seems to be presented in a straightforward manner. Whenever mentoring programs are implemented, there are many behind-the-scenes factors that can propel a program forward or squash it. This is why it can be hard to understand why some programs work and some don't. Mentoring programs are much more than a company implementation. It is more than simply adding a "did you mentor" or "do you have a mentor" checkbox to employee performance evaluations. When done correctly, mentoring comes from a vibe or culture in the organization. Culture isn't quantified; it is felt. An organization that promotes open dialogue, connections, and expressing vulnerability without judgment or negative ramifications fosters a productive mentoring environment. Mentoring, when done correctly, is characterized by a perception and cultivation driven by the leaders in the organization that model the key components of mentoring, i.e. generativity, intrinsic motivation, meaningful connections, trust, and goals. Colgate-Palmolive's research arm in New Jersey is an organization that has such a culture. Their program drives hierarchical and lateral mentoring™ by encouraging employees to meet, connect, and mentor.

Few workplaces see members' vulnerabilities as assets. These are counterintuitive to the strength and independence most companies, especially large ones, want to promote. Colgate-Palmolive, founded in 1806, is a global leader in household and personal care products. Additionally, it produces veterinary and nutritional products for pets. I met LaTonya Kilpatrick, currently the senior vice president of Clinical Research, Innovation, and Scientific Communications at Colgate Palmolive Co., around 2017, when I spoke at Colgate's Women's Network, at their research facility in New Jersey. The audience was mostly women; they all sat in pairs or groups. They were animated and didn't seem as though they were forced to be there. In fact, I found out later that no one was required to attend. Everything seemed normal. The difference between this talk and others I've experienced was the way the audience was interacting with each other. They were at ease. They weren't rushed. No one looked as if they were on a mission or just killing time at a required event.

Within the research facility at Colgate-Palmolive, the Colgate Women's Network is vital in fostering connections and allowing for vulnerability among its members. This network is thriving, which is no surprise, thanks to the encouragement and example set by its leaders.

The Women's Network provides a platform for women to connect, meet, and find mentors, which fosters a supportive community. I had the pleasure of experiencing this firsthand when I met LaTonya. As a leader, she was present at the talk. She sat with another person and took the time to talk to me and others who were present. She didn't rush back to her desk. Instead, she took more than an hour to give a tour to a colleague and me (which I did not expect) and described how all of the divisions operate. I could see scientists in lab coats behind glass walls working diligently. We even had an opportunity to learn about the research a microbiologist was working on to improve oral health. My takeaway was that everyone in research was connected to each other. There wasn't any work being done in a silo. And everyone was happy to take time to answer questions, meet someone new, and share their expertise.

The Women's Network was established in response to historical challenges women face in research, including limited upward mobility, insufficient support, and a lack of role models compared to men. The network's primary purpose is to facilitate networking opportunities, allowing women to connect within their divisions and departments. Through these interactions, members learn from one another, offer mutual support, and engage in mentorship, contributing to the network's vibrant and thriving community.

LaTonya and I continued our connection following my visit. I learned later that this is standard practice. Connections are meaningful and matter. During our conversation, she expressed her deep appreciation for mentorship, sharing stories about her own mentors and emphasizing the importance of mentoring others. She grasped the broader impact of mentoring on individuals' personal lives and professional success, including its role in driving team achievements. Shortly thereafter, LaTonya joined The Mentor Project as a mentor despite her busy schedule. Her commitment to giving back and supporting others was evident. Since then, I've been continuously learning from LaTonya, who has been a guest speaker for my undergraduate gender class at the college where I teach. Students admire her because of her approachable nature and ability to seamlessly integrate discussions about her work and family life, showcasing how women can excel as leaders at work and in their personal lives. She leads with her humanity rather than her impressive résumé.

LaTonya Kilpatrick holds a PhD in chemistry from Princeton University and has been with Colgate-Palmolive's research arm in New Jersey for decades. She is the holder of several patents and the author of many book chapters and journal articles. And she wants to share it all. She is particularly passionate about exposing young children to science. She has volunteered for a number of education-based programs sponsored by Colgate and has found that mentoring, developing meaningful connections, and having the ability to express vulnerability are keys to making her career work for her.

When we first met, I was unaware of her impressive position, .but I was struck by her willingness to engage and participate in discussions. Witnessing her interactions with others was inspiring. People were eager to connect with her, and there was a sense of pride in showcasing their work to someone of her stature. LaTonya's presence exemplified the power of leadership and empathy, leaving a lasting impression on everyone she met.

Mentoring Enhances Personal and Professional Development

A classic movie example of hierarchical mentoring is *The Karate Kid* (1984), where Mr. Miyagi mentors Daniel LaRusso in life lessons through karate. In contrast to the authoritarian and hostile teaching of a rival karate school, Miyagi shows Daniel that the proper practice of martial arts techniques imparts important values such as patience, perseverance, and self-discipline. Their mentor-mentee relationship is central to the story, showcasing how a wise and caring mentor can guide a younger person through challenges and help them grow. While this example was organically developed with the characters gaining personal development (which leads to later professional development for Daniel), the classic mentoring style of expert and novice is often applied in the workplace.

Mentorship in the research division where LaTonya works is fairly typical of hierarchical organizations in that mentors are assigned mentees. As in many organizations, mentorship is not required, but is expected and is an action item tagged for career development. Often, models like this fall flat because the motivation can be extrinsic—meaning there is an outside variable (implied requirement) driving the mentoring relationship. This often leads to resentment and a feeling of burden for mentors. But it is different in the case of Colgate-Palmolive's research division.

Leaders assign mentors to employees with the intention of helping them develop and improve their skills. The goal is to create a more effective and productive team. Mentors are identified and assigned by the leaders, and mentees are responsible for setting up initial meetings and aligning with their mentors to achieve their goals. There is a structure and protocol that both mentors and mentees know exist, which allows them to interact without feeling awkward. That is, mentees and mentors are not left to wonder whether a mentor or mentee would like to work together. Once assigned, there is a green light indicating both are ready to interact. Some organizations expect mentorship to happen, but they do not provide a clear path for making it work. As a result, mentees may feel intimidated about approaching a potential mentor, and mentors may not know whether their overture will be appreciated; they may not even know a mentee exists.

Colgate is different. They see mentoring as a way to expose employees to different networks of people as well as to new and different experiences. Sometimes, mentors are assigned just to give an employee exposure to new individuals and departments. Essentially, the idea is to expose them to new ways of thinking. It is specifically designed to get people out of their silos. Mentors aren't expected to handle work questions, strategy, or anything coaches do. They are expected to mentor as mentorship is defined—with confidential conversations allowing for vulnerability and trust. Colgate has found this to be tremendously helpful in lateral mentoring™, not just climbing the ladder. Vulnerability is expected. It isn't something to hide.

Mentorship is not a requirement, but Colgate does put mentoring on their career development ladder as an action item. As LaTonya explained, sometimes mentors are just assigned for exposure. There isn't an overarching goal to get someone to another level. Instead, the mentoring goal is to connect and expand the connections of the mentee by exposing them to a different network of people or by giving the mentee a new experience. This is a growth goal that helps when trying to solve problems. Having lateral connections, exposure, and experiences has a tremendous impact because the resources available to figure something out are exponentially greater when people connect and learn across disciplines and departments. And because they're talking to new people, a mentee has a different perspective when interacting with their own department and other departments. They can see new ways of connecting dots that can lead to completed projects and innovation. Just having that additional contact and knowledge can lead to someone acting more creatively.

Another benefit is being exposed to more people in the company. When direct reports are submitted, those individuals are seen in a new and more complex way than they were before being connected. They are often seen as people rather than as a title or rank in the company.

Leaders of departments, whether vice presidents or directors, are responsible for delivering results. They are also responsible for ensuring that their team has a development plan and that they are performing in a way that will benefit other parts of the organization. Leaders will think: "What's the plan for this person, and what activities are being identified to help them develop and improve?" Leaders assign mentors to employees to help them develop and improve their skills to create a more effective and productive team. Mentors are identified and assigned by the leaders. This differs from many organizations, where mentees are told, "Go find a mentor," making it a mentee-driven effort. In the case of Colgate, mentors are assigned to mentees, which makes it a mentor-driven relationship. As a result, mentorship is encouraged, even expected. Mentorship is part of the organization's culture, similar to that of smiling as people pass each other in the hallway. As LaTonya explained, she never experienced mentor-mentee pairings as an extrinsic motivator. It was not a burden demanded of her. Instead, she looks at it as an opportunity to connect.

Connections at work are incredibly valuable. Feeling isolated, working in isolation, or feeling uncomfortable communicating with colleagues from other departments can hinder workplace productivity. At Colgate, informal networks and mentorship programs play a crucial role, driven by colleagues' intrinsic motivation to support one another. LaTonya Kilpatrick emphasizes how these networks foster an environment where people are more inclined to say yes to mentorship requests because being approached as a mentor makes them feel appreciated and motivated. It's a source of pride rather than feeling like a burden because it signals that someone values their expertise and seeks their guidance. LaTonya emphasizes that genuine appreciation and recognition are key drivers for engaging in mentorship, highlighting it as an honor that reinforces one's sense of expertise and contribution. Employees want to be asked to mentor others as it validates their standing as recognized experts within the organization.

Informal networks add to the value of mentorship, especially lateral mentorship. As individuals meet others in organization-sponsored groups (such as the Women's Network) they see where mentorship can fit in across disciplines and divisions because they are getting a better understanding of the expertise their colleagues possess. LaTonya emphasized the importance of being personable and connecting with others. This is important for career advancement. Further, getting out of the lab and away from the computer to build meaningful connections is a game changer. People are more likely to remember and support individuals who have formed meaningful connections with others rather than choosing to simply sit alone. This is how lateral mentoring™ works. It is organic, with mentors and mentees seeking expertise and guidance from people who are not their bosses. Colgate had a connected vibe. People walk together, sit together, smile at each other, and seem connected as a whole.

Most Colgate employees have both coaching and mentoring. How do they differ? Are they actually distinguished appropriately, or is it a mishmash of coaching and mentoring principles being applied? I was pleasantly surprised to discover that coaching and mentorship are seen differently and as having separate goals. Often, mentoring and coaching are combined in an organization. In fact, many coaches I've spoken with believe they cover both mentoring and coaching when working with clients. At Colgate, coaching is about getting direction and is designed to help employees grow and learn. It is strategy-based. Mentoring, on the other hand, is about having an emotional connection and trusting the person you are sharing insights with. You can have confidential conversations with your mentor. It was particularly interesting to me that LaTonya mentioned trust because that is a key component of mentoring and, although trusting colleagues is often expected, valuing the expression of vulnerability (which can lead to trust) usually is not. There is a disconnect between what is ultimately expected and how to get there. It is difficult to trust someone if you don't feel safe showing your vulnerabilities. At Colgate, a meaningful connection was expected to come from a trusted, confidential mentoring relationship where mentor and mentee mutually share.

LaTonya explained that meaningful connections and trust are key at Colgate. You need to be able to show your vulnerability and have a goal in mind when connecting with someone you expect will help you reach those goals. You need to be able to open up to them and tell them confidentially what you are thinking and feeling. She also says it is common to seek different perspectives from multiple mentors. This helps gain a well-rounded understanding of what a mentor and mentee are looking for in solving a problem or trying to reach a goal. Offering to help, even if uncertain about the goal or how to solve a problem, is appreciated and often leads to meaningful connections at work. It also builds trust.

LaTonya finds joy in mentoring. She was introduced to her current mentee by someone she used to work with. Despite being from different departments and locations, LaTonya in New Jersey and her mentee in New York, they clicked instantly. Their conversations revealed shared interests, and LaTonya emphasizes how she not only teaches but also learns from her mentee, appreciating the unique perspectives she brings. What stands out for LaTonya is her mentee's initiative in setting meeting dates, thereby demonstrating her active engagement in the mentorship dynamic. Often, mentors tell me one of the things that bothers them is when a mentee stops contacting them. The mentor often feels a sense of loss and worries that a failure on their part led to the mentee not being proactive. In LaTonya's case, her mentee's proactive approach to setting up meetings benefited both of them. As LaTonya observes, her mentee gains as much from their interactions as she does because she keeps returning and wants to continue their relationship. This positive experience encourages them to continue their mentorship journey.

Outside of work, LaTonya mentors teenagers who come to her through The Mentor Project. She knows how important her mentors were to her and understands how important emotional support and guidance can be for mentees. This is the case whether you are trying to figure out what you want to do with the rest of your life, whether you want to figure out how to get a problem solved at work, or whether you want to get to the next level at work.

Professional Services

What comes to mind when you are asked to envision a leader? Is it a person who is above all others? Someone in charge with many strengths? Leadership is seen a bit differently by Dr. Quintin McGrath, a former global senior managing director with a large global professional services firm with more than 25 years of experience. He was three levels away from reporting to the global CEO. He was a mentor in the organization who noticed a cultural shift over the past two decades, including a flattening of the hierarchy, resulting in more collaborative leadership. He credits much of this to the leadership taking on a purpose-driven approach and encouraging more lateral mentoring™ than the traditional hierarchical mentoring method many of us are most familiar with. As a result, his firm became less strictly hierarchical, i.e. with a top boss communicating in a straight line down, from one level to another. The change was due, in part, to the growth in the consulting component of the firm, which influenced the organization's culture.

The culture change included a mentoring, coaching and sponsoring approach designed to support diverse employees. The firm took an approach that borrowed from diversity initiatives across various countries, including India, Germany, and the United States. The traditional hierarchical, silo, approach doesn't work when you are trying to accomplish goals globally; mentoring was a key to flattening the usual hierarchy.

Quintin was very focused on mentoring. A lot of his mentoring was tied into his managerial role and mentoring was relayed to those on his team. He saw this shift in the mentoring and leadership culture beginning 10 or 15 years ago. At that time, his organization began to add mentoring to leadership roles. Leadership morphed from a "get this done" orientation and became more person-based, supporting the individual wherever they were in the hierarchy. This is the definition of lateral mentoring™. As Quintin describes it, "Think about mentoring outside of a hierarchy and start mentoring in terms of supporting the individual." He recalls that the shift in the workplace began when millennials started entering the workforce. A different mindset came in with them. They were open to and even expected to be mentored. This new employee generation did not want a leader as a manager but a leader who could also mentor them to success. The journey has moved so far that now individuals can speak with a manager as a peer, which removes a lot of the vulnerability and trust issues present with hierarchical leadership and mentorship. The hierarchy begins to flatten when employees trust those above them to help, rather than judge them, when they have questions. And, not so incidentally, morale and performance improve. It's a win-win.

The way it worked was mentorship and leadership intersected to help professionals solve problems and climb the corporate ladder. The focus shifted from individual recognition to contributing effectively as a team player. The firm's purpose-driven approach of making a positive impact on individuals, teams, clients, and society will get an individual employee and a team further than going it alone. Mentoring is the glue that makes this approach work.

Quintin McGrath emphasized mentoring as a way to help individuals grow and develop their skills rather than being intimidated by the vulnerability and anxiety most of us have when we are faced with learning something new. The mentor-driven approach, with mentors identifying strengths and growth areas in their mentees, helps to reduce these negative feelings. After all, a growth area sounds much better than a weakness, and we all have room to grow. As the classic adage puts it: "You can catch more flies with honey than with vinegar." Quintin believes that mentoring within an organization is important for professional growth and capability development, which means that leaders should be mentoring their team members to help them grow and succeed. This leadership plan moves whole teams forward; a positive by-product is that the individuals move up as well. His motivation to mentor is to help his team members develop professionally and to build a strong team that can operate effectively to drive the organization's success.

This approach helps to solidify a team rather than divide it as it might in a traditional hierarchical setting. As teams build mentorship into the core of their leadership, the team becomes unified rather than divided and competitive with one another. They no longer need to be vying with their fellow team members to climb to the next rung on the ladder. Mentoring teams help a team work as a unit so that all can move up, which fosters lateral as well as hierarchical mentoring. This strategy gets individuals to work together and seek out support, knowledge, and wisdom from colleagues whose strengths mitigate their weaknesses. It removes the vulnerability associated with asking someone for help because they are not competing with you for promotions. They are working with you to your mutual benefit. In traditional, hierarchical mentoring, it is more difficult to seek guidance from someone you think may be competing with you for a promotion or from a boss.

The way Quintin sees it, leadership and mentorship are intertwined, with a focus on both team strength and individual growth. This is because when leaders see the value of mentorship in a lateral sense, employee intimidation is removed, and team members are empowered to shine. The excitement of individuals on teams mentoring each other makes them all feel like winners when their team succeeds. An organization needs some level of hierarchy, of course. Someone needs to have decision-making power. However, the way the firm operates has definitely shifted it to a flatter organization. This is due in large part to the mentoring component, which is embedded in the leadership role.

This approach is not limited to professional services and consulting firms. I've seen it when I've spoken with tech entrepreneurs and when I interviewed Bill Cheswick, who described how Bell Labs approached innovation in the workplace by encouraging mentorship among colleagues. In both cases, there was a flattening of the hierarchy, with lateral mentorship driving people to innovate because the goal was to solve a problem rather than move up a career ladder. The motivation wasn't about a desire to become the boss but to create something that made a change or a difference. As in Bell Labs and other innovation think tanks, promotion and hierarchical status at large global professional services firms, as Quintin experienced it, was based on valid knowledge strengths rather than status strength, as it would be in a more traditional hierarchy. This leads to an atmosphere of more communication among levels and across divisions.

The rapid growth of the consulting component of the organization is another factor that led to the greater use of lateral mentoring™ approaches there. The organization's culture and leadership style have become more collaborative and team-focused. Mentoring became an expectation from incoming consultants as they were brought onto teams and were required to contribute effectively. Consultants were not just mentored on how the organization operates and how to onboard effectively but also on how to get the best from the individuals they were working with. They needed to be fully integrated. Mentoring on diversity, equity, and inclusion was important for the global organization as individuals were working with people from all over the world. It was a mindset shift with mentoring at the helm. This free exchange of information between individuals who may not have communicated freely before was a big burst for lateral mentoring™ and for flattening the hierarchy. Consulting opened the door for less traditional mentoring and leadership to take place, which was transformative for the organization.

This mentoring approach also allows room for modern approaches to mentoring, such as AI-driven information utilization. Quintin explained that AI can help provide information that, in the past, might have been obtained only from a mentor but can now be obtained through AI bots and other AI information sources. This will likely become even more prevalent as AI continues to develop. Quintin believes AI can facilitate knowledge sharing and collaboration (and lateral mentorship) in a flattened organizational structure, allowing for more efficient and effective learning. AI can serve as the "synapse area," connecting two teams together, two ideas together, or two concepts together, making it easier to bring them together and learn from one another.

Quintin believes that leadership has evolved from a master-apprentice dynamic, which is the hierarchical model, to a more communal focus, where leaders serve and work together with others. The service leader, whose goal is to serve the team and the organization, is "other-focused" rather than self-focused. This creates a flatter organizational structure—a lateral structure, which shifts the model from a service-oriented organization (hierarchical) approach to a lateral one. Individuals are recognized and rewarded if they are able to make their team more effective. Mentorship becomes woven in as part of the organization's fabric rather than as an add-on. Individuals ask, "How do I contribute most effectively; how can I better understand my weaknesses and someone else's strengths?" This is a key in lateral mentoring™, which makes it the perfect model of mentoring to flatten a hierarchical leadership model.

The approach to mentoring for Quintin is asking himself, "How can I play my part where I'm seen as an incredibly good player?" He also asks those he is looking to mentor, "What is driving you at work today?" and "Why do you want to be at work?" Quintin is looking for their purpose. He wants to find meaning in himself and help others to do the same. He wants to know he is making a positive impact at work and with his mentees. He asks his mentees, "Are you making a positive impact, and what are the things you are doing that actually make an impact that matters?" He wants to help his mentees find the places they can make a significant contribution, which, of course, feeds right into purpose and meaning. As a leader, mentoring in this way, he helps those he is leading and mentoring to become a part of a vision for the team, with an individual role to play in making that vision a reality. Quintin is always looking to fan sparks of genuine growth. He then looks to feed that spark by providing the skills and opportunities that allow the spark to grow into a roaring flame.

This form of mentoring is mentor-driven rather than mentee-driven. The mentor is looking for mentees to support, and looking to expand strengths and diminish weaknesses. Traditional hierarchical mentoring is often led by the mentee who is searching for support and guidance. When mentoring is mentor-driven, the mentor is motivated to mentor because it is initiated by them. There is no extrinsic motivation, such as job expectation, raise, praise, or promotion, attached to the mentoring. It is genuinely intrinsic.

The idea of changing how we look at leadership, with mentorship as a key component, shifts the purpose of employees from serving themselves to serving the organization and colleagues. It shifts the focus away from what is good for me toward what best serves the greater good. Mentorship, when it is lateral in a hierarchical environment, helps flatten the leadership model to make everyone more accessible and increases the positive impact for all.

Military

Mentorship is not a luxury in the military. It is crucial for growth, success, and survival.

Imagine how it feels to know that your mentor can guide you not only in the hierarchy of your career but also in life-and-death situations. That is, whether you live or die could depend on your mentor-mentee relationship. So a lot is riding on it. As of 2023, the US military employed over 2.8 million personnel globally. Now imagine those 2.8 million people accomplishing life-and-death feats without guidance, trust, and meaningful connections. Mentorship is vital in the military.

It is valued, and it is expected. And it is necessary.

The Importance of Mentorship

Jennifer Snow, a retired Lieutenant Colonel in the United States Air Force, served as a Special Operations Command intelligence officer, chief technology officer for AFWERX (the Air Force Innovation arm) and is currently on the board of directors of The Mentor Project. During our discussion on mentoring, she shared a touching anecdote about her time as a commissioned officer, highlighting the profound impact one of her mentors, Lt. Colonel Brad Thompson, had on her. Lt. Colonel Thompson's mentorship not only guided her career progression but also imparted valuable lessons on mentorship itself. He crafted a letter for her (Figure 7.1), detailing insights designed to help her understand her leadership role and navigate the responsibilities of an officer, while also excelling as an intelligence analyst. This letter, preserved since 2005, remains a poignant reminder of the significance of his mentorship. Jennifer emphasized how each line in the letter remains relevant and significant, showcasing Lt. Colonel Thompson's thoughtful guidance tailored to her needs as a leader and mentor.

Feedback / Expectations for Lt Snow.   Sep 2005
From: Lt col Thompson

* By virtue of your rank, you automatically become a Senior leader in our Sqdn. We have a very young officer corps in the Sqd -- please expect to live up to this expectation; be a leader. You are an officer 1st, Intel analyst 2d

* There is no us and them in our Sqdn i.e. Combat Support vs operators; don't allow it to happen. See it -- Fix it

* Accountability of self and everything you do, your programs/products

* You'll be #2 in Intel, but support your boss and step up and take repsonsibility

* Ensure you fight for feedback and give feedback up and down -- one of the most important things we do as officers.

* Support your Sqdn leadership -- your office reports to DO (major Platten). 720 STG should never task you directly -- don't let it happen -- if it does -- fix it and let your chain of command know.

* Govt card -- never be late period whether you are paid or not -- as an officer -- you can only lose.

* No sexual harassment in our Sqdn; zero tolerance by you; plus don't tolerate it if you see it -- report it to chain of command. We are trying to foster a Safe, enjoyable and mission focused Sqdn -- I'm fostering "team building."

* Alcohol : there is none allowed in our Sqdn; you see it -- address it

* Read OI's + Policy Letters all found in OSS

* Be prepared to deploy at all times; keep your life in order

FIGURE 7.1 Letter from mentor Lt. Colonel Thompson.

The military is well known to be a hierarchical environment in which leadership and trust are fundamental. Most people can readily think of ways in which a mentee needs to trust a mentor. But rarely is the trust of a mentee by a mentor discussed. Mentors in the military must trust their mentees because the mentor-mentee relationship may have life-and-death consequences. The structure may be hierarchical,

See Cannington to accomplish a mobility folder a.s.o.p.

* Families are always welcome here (unless something is classif)
  Encourage and instill this in your shop

* Safety/ORM: Mission is 1st but we live ORM; practice it
  in all we do. It's empowered in every person in
  this Sqdn up and down to ensure it happens
        -- Nothing is ever administrative or admin
        in our business -- Ever!

* Always know the whereabouts of your shop -- accountability is
  big here.

* Mentorship = Never miss a chance; as an officer -- never not
  in charge and nothing is ever off the record.

* Find someone you can emulate and be someone
  others can emulate; be an example and role model

* Keep your work area spotless -- says a lot about you

* PT = most precious part of the duty day; try hard
  not to let anything interfere with that time; don't
  schedule things unless absolutely necessary

* Never let me be surprised

* No visitors unannounced to our Sqdn; stop by and
  introduce to me; next in line if I'm not there.

* Have goals and vision and tell people what they are.
  Tell people what you want in life, where you want to
  go, what you stand for.... Take care of your future and
  your records.

* Never turn down an assignment.. It's not about you; think
  bigger picture. Support AF CORE Values

* Start something of savings plan / investment plan now

* About yourself

* Questions?

        Bradley P. Thompson

FIGURE 7.1 (Continued)

but the trust has to be mutual. Both parties must be able to trust each other completely, or terrible things may happen. This is exemplified in the letter Jennifer Snow received from Lt. Colonel Thompson about trust and responsibility, which emphasizes the importance of taking on additional duties and showing reliability in small tasks.

Jennifer Snow's journey began with a deep-rooted sense of patriotism instilled by her upbringing. Raised in a Catholic household, she learned morals and values that guided her life. After undergraduate degrees and enjoying a fulfilling federal civilian job in the U.S. Fish and Wildlife Service (UFWS), her life took a pivotal turn with the tragic events of 9/11. The impact of the terrorist attack stirred a profound sense of duty within her, compelling her to contribute actively to her country's safety. Motivated by this calling, she made the life-changing decision to join the military, aspiring to serve as an intelligence officer.

Trust and Responsibility

Jen's entry into the military marked the start of a remarkable chapter in her life. Assigned to the prestigious Air Force Special Operations Command, she found herself in an elite environment, a significant achievement for a recent graduate from intelligence school. Amid the challenges and responsibilities of her new role, she encountered invaluable mentorship from figures including General Paul V. Hester, then the lead general of the Air Force Special Operations Command. General Hester's leadership style had a marked personal touch. He always took time to talk with people he passed in the hallway, and he knew everyone in the building, most of them by their first names.

It was 2003. Everyone had additional duties outside their regularly assigned jobs that kept the place running and functioning. Some jobs were better than others, and some were less than pleasant. Jennifer's fell into what most of us would consider to be the less than pleasant category. Her job was to clean the ladies' bathroom. This was before they had contract cleaners loading toilet paper and paper towels and emptying the garbage. Jennifer was responsible for taking out the trash and ensuring everything was clean and well-stocked. She decided she would do the job to the best of her ability because the principles of service for the Air Force are service before self, integrity first, and excellence in all we do. She told herself she was going to follow these core tenets and keep the bathroom as clean as she could.

Jennifer really wanted to be assigned to the 720th Special Tactics group. Although they rotated the lieutenants around so they could get experience with different units, some units were really high-pressure, and people's lives depended on the information being shared. Those who got those assignments needed to pay close attention to detail and operate at a very high level. She really wanted that job.

When General Hester came down to talk to everyone in her group, it was really eye-opening because he said, "You know, all of you have been given little tasks, additional duties to do. Some of you don't really think too much of that. And some people complain about the additional duties. But it's insightful to me because the people who did well at those duties are revealing something to me. They're telling me something important. I can trust them." He went on to say, "And you see, if I can't trust you in little things, how can I possibly trust you with the big things where people's lives are on the line?" This was a great mentoring moment. General Hester made a very clear point about trust that stuck with Jen. Mentors need to trust their mentees, and as a mentee, it was her responsibility to make certain that her mentor could trust her. And, of course, she got the assignment she wanted. She was thrilled to go to the Special Tactics group, and she credits this with being able to build trust with her mentor. And sparkly toilets.

Leadership and trust remained important features for Jennifer Snow as she advanced in her career, was mentored, and became a mentor to others. Leading by example was one of the first things she learned, which is a common practice in the military. Physical fitness examples abound, with leaders mentoring others by leading push-up exercises each day. This may seem trivial, but it is not. Seeing your mentor lead by example is powerful. You know they aren't just passing stuff off to others. They value what they are asking their mentees to do. Jennifer learned that you don't ask someone to do something without being willing to do it yourself and that leading by example is the best way to lead. Leadership doesn't have to include mentorship, but when it does, it leads to longstanding relationships and deep understanding, as with the letter Jennifer received from her mentor, Lt. Colonel Thompson. He made her feel valued, and she internalized what he said in person and in the letter. In times of stress, mentors are the people Jennifer would turn to because they helped alleviate the stress—because she trusted them and felt meaningfully connected to them despite being subordinate. Rank did not trump trust. In the military, trust is the most important factor there is, because you may be deployed or be placed in a position of vulnerability as part of your job. A leader can send you to do something, but a mentor is someone you can trust to stand by their mentees' sides and not let them fail.

Lateral Mentoring™

In the military, mentors expect their mentees to improve and grow. As a good military mentor, Jennifer Snow expected her mentees to succeed; she felt herself a failure when she didn't deliver and/ or when her mentees did not succeed. This is how her mentors felt, too. Success for a mentor is personal. When your mentee succeeds, it is a reflection on you, and a piece of the mentor is carried on through their success. The same with failures. A piece of the mentor fails right along with them. Sharing knowledge and experiences is also really important in the military. Getting to know others and getting new experiences in new places and with new people helps to keep ideas flowing and leads to success-ful problem-solving in crises. When mentors and mentees move around in the military, they retain their old connections and build new ones through new mentors.

When a problem needs to be solved or a crisis erupts, mentors and mentees can connect laterally with those who have moved on to new experiences. Long-term successful relationships are built this way. Mutual help and support manifest themselves in lateral mentoring™ relationships with people who already know and trust each other from working together on different teams. This is particularly true during deployment. Individuals don't have the time to try to gain trust and foster meaningful connections when deployed to a new location. Those mentor and mentee relationships can be found all over the place and, in deployment, individuals can find people they already know, trust, and have meaningful connections with. This makes crisis work more efficient and allows problem-solving to occur quickly. This familiarity eliminates the need to navigate emotions and new territory with strangers. There is new territory, but there are no strangers in it, and the emotions associated with them are familiar.

Safety

Understandably, safety is on the minds of the vast majority of deployed military personnel. Mentors help their mentees develop that sense of safety through gestures that matter. From showing up to bringing pizza to remote work environments, mentoring in the military often means being present in words and actions. Teammates are encouraged to look out for each other, which comes from mentors who show the importance of caring for others, even if the other person may never know you are doing it.

An example Jennifer describes occurred when she was deployed and was one of the only women on the base. She went to use the gym late at night and saw shadows—someone moving between the buildings in the dark and following her. She remained watchful and finally arrived at the gym, where she learned the shadows were two of her teammates who ensured she arrived safely. They didn't tell her, and they weren't told to do this. But, mentors teach their mentees to act on their sense of care for their teammates and to think about them even when no one will recognize what they've done. She felt grateful for her teammates' efforts to ensure her safety and create a sense of family despite the challenges of being in a new and dangerous environment.

Most of us think of the military as strictly hierarchical, and that is partly true. The military is set up in a hierarchy with leaders and mentors guiding those who are subordinate. But that's not the end of the story. Collaboration and mentorship are encouraged across divisions, especially in times of crisis, and it is all set up by the way the military shapes the thinking of its personnel. Enlistees and officers are both encouraged to try new experiences. People are deployed or placed in different divisions fairly regularly. The term "army brat" comes from a child growing up in a military family and moving around all the time. This isn't some arbitrary policy. It isn't done because the military believes in or doesn't care about uprooting individuals. It is essential for creating the ideal conditions for lateral mentoring™ and collaboration needed in times of crisis and danger.

During stable times, the military is very hierarchical, but as soon as a crisis or a problem arises, the hierarchical walls come down, and lateral mentoring™ kicks into high gear. People communicate across teams and divisions to quickly assess a situation, send information, and work to solve a problem or to strategize about how to solve said problem. If the hierarchical walls remained, this communication could not happen or would be seriously degraded. The trust built up between people when they are on a team becomes strong; they are just like a family. When individuals move to new teams, their former teammates take their trust and meaningful connections with them. They are, therefore, able to ask those individuals for information and skill sharing, support, and guidance. Once a problem is solved, the hierarchical walls go back up, and everyone goes back to working within their own teams. This flexibility allows our military personnel to pivot, reach out, and solve serious problems in a very short amount of time. It is one of the reasons our military functions so well, better than the militaries of most other nations. The core of mentoring (generativity, intrinsic motivation, meaningful connections, trust, and goals that work in any direction needed) is what makes this happen. The military isn't a one-way highway; it is a web of intricate, meaningfully connected mentors and mentees who operate at a high level every day. This cross-functional lateral mentoring™ occurs because of the tremendously high stakes; people are literally at risk of dying. This model is not unique to life-and-death situations, however. It can work anywhere, even when the stakes are not nearly as high.

Trust is a safe space, a refuge, where ideas can be shared without fear of judgment or retribution. Attachment theory, a major model in psychology, literally refers to this kind of feeling as a "secure base." Trust is necessary for psychological safety. On one occasion, she discovered that the gear they had issued her was a size too large and would get caught on vehicle doors, or the too big helmet would slip down over her eyes, making it hard to see and uncomfortable to wear in the desert heat. One of her teammates pulled together all of the extra pouches, webbing, helmet padding and harnesses the team had and crafted a set of gear that was sized to fit her smaller frame so that her vision wasn't obstructed and she wasn't tripping or constantly getting caught on wires and other equipment getting in and out of various vehicles. In this case trust was built further with her team because they wanted to make sure she had the right gear. Her teammates went out of their way to hand craft gear that would fit her to ensure she had what she needed. Most often, trust is the first key component that will be assessed when a person is looking for a mentor or mentee. Can they trust them? Will they be safe? Safety and trust go together like peanut butter and jelly. If trust isn't gained, mentorship will not succeed.

Lack of mentorship leads to the repetition of mistakes. This is why it is essential to get the key components of mentoring in place in the military. The safety of teams and individuals is at stake, and making the same mistake more than once can be very costly, even deadly. Mentors in the military prioritize empathy and helping people find their path (being generative) rather than punishing failures. Successful resolution of issues occurs when mentors are generative and look outside themselves to help others.

Crisis situations can teach valuable lessons for mentoring and teamwork. Nothing focuses the mind like a crisis, if one is prepared to face it. Open communication in a hierarchical environment is key to successful teamwork. If the hierarchical wall remains up, people will have difficulty openly communicating. If that happens, new ideas, innovation, and information may not be shared, which can lead to an inability to solve complex problems. Leaders set the tone for collaborative and team-oriented mentorship. Mentorship is best viewed as both hierarchical and lateral, with mentors and mentees investing in each other and looking out for those above, below, and alongside them.

Wall Street

Brian Martin spent 16 years on Wall Street. Originally from Canada, he was one of seven students in his college graduation class from Queen's University in Kingston, Ontario, Canada, who emigrated to the United States, and he hasn't looked back. When he was young, he was always at the top of his class, and he enjoyed problem-solving. He assumed he'd go on to college to major in premed because that is what he assumed all smart kids did. He figured cardiology would be his area of focus. But a mentor advised him against becoming a physician. This mentor told Brian that a physician is always listening to problems (which Brian was okay with), but they also had to address complaint after complaint, patient after patient, every day. She explained to him that people don't go to doctors unless they have a complaint. This did not appeal to Brian. His mentor understood that Brian, though smart and talented at solving problems, probably wasn't suited for a job as a physician. They thought about other options. Brian loved math and problem-solving, so Brian concluded that Wall Street was his calling.

One of the first things Brian learned while working on Wall Street was that people "eat what they kill." Mentoring was not on his radar. It wasn't even a concept to him, and he wasn't alone in this kind of thinking. One day at work, Brian asked a colleague how he got the contacts for a company. The colleague, who was always friendly and polite, turned to him and said: "Why would I tell you that?" Brian was taken aback. He thought, "Why wouldn't he?" Then it dawned on him. The colleague thought Brian would take his clients or find a way to outsmart him and get his position. This colleague was one rung above him on the hierarchical ladder. Clearly, the climate was cutthroat such that sharing information was a no-no. Generativity apparently wasn't an option on Wall Street.

Brian did find a mentor when he was at CitiGroup through a person who served as a lateral mentor™ but wasn't part of his company. This mentor, Nima Ghamsari, taught Brian computer languages that could be used to bridge divisions under one operating system. Nima noticed that Brian was not a gifted trader or investor. He helped Brian see that he had a true knack for innovating and that he was good at bringing technologies together and making them work more efficiently. This was an aha moment for Brian and helped him see his role in the workspace differently, which led him to pivot to other areas of Wall Street, i.e. learning skills involving technology.

After 16 years, Brian exited Wall Street to work with his former mentor, Nima, who had started a company, called Blend. Brian contacted Nima and said, "So I don't know what you're doing. I don't know what kind of company you are starting. But I know that you're one of the most visionary people I've ever met. When you need a businessperson at your company, call me first." Brian waited about a year and half and joined as the 57th employee of the start-up Blend, which went from zero to $350 million in revenue in five-and-a-half years.

At this point, Brian split from Nima to form his own company, Pine (online mortgage and lending company), which has been called the Canadian version of the US company Rocket Mortgage.

Mentoring in Wall Street wasn't entirely hierarchical. You could find lateral mentors™ from different divisions or companies, but within your own division and company, it barely existed. The fear of someone taking your job, clients, or money was always in the back of the minds of everyone. It may sound harsh, but like hunting, if you don't come home with anything, you won't eat. Everyone wanted to eat.

Brian acknowledged that entrepreneurship is a whole different ball game with regard to mentorship. People are excited to help others and tend to be naturally generative. It was after he became an entrepreneur that he decided to join The Mentor Project and now sits on its board of directors. He mentors students, mentors me, and is a member of the Innovation Lab, where students learn how to innovate and get their ideas into the world. It is a long way from his "eat what you kill" days.

Big Law Firms

Jura Zibas is an equity partner and co-chair of the Intellectual Property practice at Wilson Elser, a law firm with more than 1,000 employees in 44 offices in the United States and one in London. Jura didn't set out to become a lawyer. She wanted to be a dentist. After she graduated from Tulane University, she attended dental school at Ohio State University. When she graduated, she realized that she didn't want to practice dentistry, so she set her sights on and worked her way through law school at Capital University in Columbus, Ohio. Along the way, she passed the patent bar and when she graduated, took the first job that came her way—as a public defender. She got great trial experience and had terrific mentors who gave her advice and guided her along the way to learn the nuances of a trial, as well as putting together a case. Her years as a public defender in the early 1990s provided her with some of the best mentors in her law career. She was openly vulnerable, and they felt comfortable giving her tough feedback when needed. It wasn't a time filled with coddling and pats on the back. It was a time to make a mistake once, get some good guidance from a senior lawyer, and learn. Each mistake she made, followed by guidance from her mentors, helped hone her skills as a trial lawyer. The one-on-one mentorship she received from judges and senior lawyers was vital to her career. It was hands-on, direct, and hierarchical.

After a few years as a public defender, Jura moved to New York City to expand her options. She took any job she could find; she even took a two-year stint in Silicon Valley. Jura has a unique background in science, technology, and as a trial attorney. New firms recruited her after seeing her in action, during a trial. Trials seemed to be her "interviews" for jobs. She climbed the ladder and ultimately landed at Wilson Elser, a giant firm that grossed more than $395 million in 2022. She is still there today and has made partner. She is widely respected in her field, and with years of practice under her belt, she gives back. She mentors at work, though mentoring is vastly different than when she was a public defender. She is also a founding member of The Mentor Project. She came on board because of her desire to mentor in STEM. She did all of the legal work for The Mentor Project, mentors the mentors, and mentors students who are pursuing patents. We wouldn't be an organization without her. She devoted hours to getting us off the ground, helping us become a nonprofit, file papers, and trademark our name.

Formal mentoring programs in big law firms are described by Jura as ineffective. In her words, "Nowadays, mentorship is more artificial and less effective due to lack of honesty and dialogue." Mentoring at her firm is offered in groups by an assigned mentor. The mentors aren't always interested in mentoring (though some are). It is a requirement. The mentees meet in a group with one mentor, and no one shares. It isn't a safe environment because no one feels they can be openly vulnerable, they don't trust anyone, and there aren't any meaningful connections. The atmosphere is similar to what Brian Martin described as "you eat what you kill," and no one wants to be seen as vulnerable or share what they've taken time and energy to learn. It is not an effective mentoring model. It is strictly hierarchical, and trust is at a minimum.

In Jura's opinion, formal mentoring programs are ineffective. Organic mentoring is another story, however. That, she believes, is effective, and that is how she tries to operate. She takes on one-on-one mentees, guiding them as she was once mentored when she worked as a public defender. She allows her mentees to make mistakes and works to make sure they learn from those mistakes. Before becoming the mentor she is now, she used to fix their mistakes and pass it through. The mentees didn't learn, and mistakenly felt that they were moving ahead on their own. This wasn't always helpful. Mentoring is a skill she has honed over the years, and embracing mistakes is one thing she feels helps mentees grow (it also bonds them, as they have come to her to thank her for allowing them to learn from their mistakes). Jura has found that trust and connections are key to the mentoring she does, and feels trust, connections, intrinsic motivation, and generativity are all missing in the group mentoring that is required at the firm.

Jura has had to create her own ways to mentor at her job as the model they have in place is not conducive to productive mentoring. She finds mentees at work, develops relationships with them, and guides them, but it is not part of a formal program in any way. Nor is it part of her job. She also mentors within The Mentor Project. Mentoring, for Jura, is something she does—and will find a way to engage in. She is built to do it.

Health Care

Hospitals and health care environments are known for being hierarchical work habitats. Rank and degree of employees are synonymous with their level and power. I met Dr. Miriam Bredella at a mentoring engagement in 2022 at Mass General Hospital (MGH), a Harvard hospital. I was the keynote speaker talking about lateral mentoring™ in a hierarchical environment.

Miriam, a professor of radiology at Harvard Medical School for nearly 20 years, became the vice chair of faculty affairs at Mass General Hospital in 2018. And the first thing her chair asked her to do was to establish a mentoring program for the faculty, which they did not have at that point. Dr. Bredella was responsible for the careers of 3,000 faculty members and 4,000 research scientists. This does not even include the postdocs and graduate students.

When Miriam started her career at Harvard, she realized that it was a little different than other medical schools because you start out as an instructor rather than as an assistant professor. Promotion is important. You're already a rank below other institutions, and Miriam noticed that if people don't get the professor in their title and remain instructor, they are more likely to leave. She thought mentorship might be a really good idea. For her it was not just that people need a mentor to feel good about their job. A big part for her was to help people to get the academic promotion they all craved. She realized that, at Harvard, no one really looked out for you. You could be an instructor for the rest of your life. No one really cared. But there was also no one who pushed you. She decided to do something about that.

Miriam's goal was to create a program that involved people who cared. She wanted mentors who would actually look at someone's curriculum vitae and help them navigate to the next level. It wasn't that people were mean or uncaring, but there were all sorts of problems that held people back from getting to the next level. Unless a person was really driven, it was difficult to overcome the many obstacles to making it to the next level. This was especially true for women. Many were just too burdened by clinical work to do anything else. First time attendings are just starting families, have young children, so making it through the day is difficult enough without thinking about promotions. Miriam decided she would focus on junior faculty. They were the most vulnerable and most in need of a mentor to help them cut through the overwhelming impediments that most junior faculty face.

She set up a program whose goal was to bring in mentors who could take a look at junior faculty's curriculum vitae, tell them what they needed for promotion, and help them reach those goals by giving professional talks and publishing papers. Her mentoring program turned out to be very successful. Within a year, twice as many people got promoted than in prior years. People also reported feeling more connected. The program didn't just focus on promotion. The junior faculty mentees felt more connected and believed someone cared for them.

In a hierarchical environment, such as a hospital or academic medicine, there is a risk of being overlooked and feeling disconnected. A mentor is a connection that can not only support and guide but be a grounding source for a mentee who is feeling overwhelmed. In Miriam's case, adding a mentoring program helped the institution as much as it did the mentees. Promotions mean employees are doing their jobs well and, in this case, mentors helped double the number of instructors who received promotions. The simple act of caring and providing insight into navigating to the next career step was all that was needed to make an enormous impact. Again, a win-win.

Mentoring is a constant presence in the workplace, wending its way through even the most fiercely competitive environments. Each workplace paints its unique picture of mentoring, ranging from hierarchical structures to more horizontal or lateral relationships. Some are better organized and more effective than others, depending on their understanding and use of the key components of mentoring: generativity, intrinsic motivation, meaningful connections, trust, and goals. But regardless of the setting and of the quality of mentoring, all workplaces engage in mentoring, shaping growth, and fostering connections (or not). Recognizing and appreciating the diverse styles of mentoring and knowing how to set up effective mentoring programs is key. When done well, mentoring empowers individuals to navigate varying scenarios with finesse, crafting tailored mentoring approaches that enhance productivity and nurture a supportive workplace culture. Understanding these nuances not only enriches the mentor-mentee experience but can also transform the workplace into a thriving ecosystem where mentorship thrives, contributing to collective success and individual fulfillment. The ultimate win-win.

Moving from the practical application of mentorship in the workplace, our focus in the next chapter shifts toward a research-driven exploration of mentorship's essence. Defining mentorship through research requires a comprehensive examination of its dynamics, benefits, and challenges across different scenarios. The aim is to unravel the intricacies of mentorship from the perspective of the mentor and the mentee. A scholarly approach unravels the complexities of mentorship, enabling us to harness its transformative potential.

8

Defining Mentoring through Research

Before establishing The Mentor Project, I examined mentorship through the lens of Erik Erikson's theory of generativity. As mentioned in a previous chapter, this developmental life stage is about an emotional desire to give back to others without expecting anything from them in return. It is a desire, even a need, to have a legacy. When I was exploring this idea, in the early 2000s, discussions about mentoring were not widespread, and convincing individuals of the value of mentors was challenging. When I spoke with people, particularly those aged 20 to 40, they tended to view mentorship as a one-sided exchange. In their minds, an anonymous, unseen mentor bestowed wisdom and opened doors for the mentee. The mentee was the focus, and the mentor was the afterthought. The primary objective was for a person to become a mentee—they were to find a generous mentor and extract personal gain to advance their interests. Any thought about the gain or value in this relationship for the mentor was not part of the equation. This perspective almost made it seem as if mentees were akin to thieves, swiftly seizing valuable insights from unsuspecting mentors. However, I saw something different. I saw this relationship from the vantage point of the mentor. I became fascinated by the connection between mentoring and generativity. I realized that mentors, possessing expertise and a desire to impart it, were the driving force behind meaningful mentoring relationships. They were not simply benefiting the mentee; the mentor benefited by having a mentee. It was a two-way street, with the mentor getting at least as much from the relationship as the mentee. I decided to see whether I was right.

I conducted interviews with over 40 mentors, ranging from a four-star general to a grandmother who had experience as a mentor. What struck me was their shared understanding of the value and benefits they gained from their mentorship experiences. They were quite aware of the benefits they received from the fulfillment they felt in mentoring. While their individual stories varied, they consistently highlighted five key components of effective mentoring that have been discussed throughout this book:

1. **Generativity**: The desire to contribute to and positively influence others.
2. **Intrinsic motivation**: An internal drive to engage in mentoring beyond external rewards.
3. **Meaningful connections**: Building relationships that go beyond mere transactional exchanges.
4. **Trust**: Feeling trusted and trusting the other. A fundamental element for successful mentor-mentee interactions.
5. **Goal setting**: Establishing clear objectives and working collaboratively toward them.

My intuition crystallized into a mission. To understand how mentorship truly operates, I needed to weave together theoretical concepts from research with insights from real-world mentors. I had to integrate what the research literature said with what real mentors had shared with me. Neither the existing literature nor my interviews alone fully captured the perspective of benefits to the mentor. I needed to explore this dynamic further by integrating the two. The results are the creation of an organization to match mentors with mentees (The Mentor Project) and this book. The former to put my findings into practical action; the latter to document what I learned.

If I think of defining mentoring and where we are with it today, a few terms come to mind: loosely defined, applied widely, anecdotal, and disconnected. A few decades ago, the term "mentor" was scarcely used. People weren't actively seeking mentors at work, nor were they discussing mentorship programs. Today, however, mentorship is everywhere, and new definitions pop up all the time. Most recently, I saw mutual mentorship in a conference panel title. I have no idea what mutual mentorship means, and, unfortunately, the panelists didn't either. Mentorship is applied widely, almost as a catchall. It has become a prominent term in academia, corporate environments, and community initiatives. It is a check box requirement, but it is often underutilized and misunderstood. I've also noticed components of mentoring are talked about in a disconnected way—hierarchical mentoring is virtually never differentiated from lateral mentoring™. Professional mentoring is rarely differentiated from and/or connected to personal mentorship. Definitions matter. We need to know what we are talking about if we are to apply it productively. A synthesized, scientific understanding of mentorship is needed to define, differentiate, combine, and apply all aspects of mentorship. Only then can we all benefit from what mentorship has to offer.

Anecdotal evidence has shed light on the need for mentoring. One popular anecdote that highlights the importance of mentoring is the story of Steve Jobs and his mentor, Bill Campbell. Steve Jobs, the cofounder of Apple Inc., often credited Bill Campbell, a former CEO of Intuit, as a mentor who played a significant role in Jobs's career development. This emphasizes how even very successful leaders benefit from mentorship. This illustrates how mentorship can have a profound impact on an individual's personal and professional growth, regardless of how successful they are. But anecdotes alone are insufficient. To truly address the issue of mentorship and enhance its effectiveness, we must also understand it scientifically. Consider weather prediction: In the past, people relied on observations of the sky, moon, and even cow behavior to predict weather patterns. However, it was only when weather science became formalized that we could implement systems to understand weather phenomena, prevent disasters, and anticipate hurricanes, heat waves, and rainfall.

Similarly, transforming anecdotal information about mentorship into a scientific framework allows us to assess existing evidence, identify gaps, and chart a path forward. Just as scientific weather forecasting saves lives by preparing for extreme weather events, a scientific approach to mentoring can help us improve emotional well-being and effectiveness for individuals and organizations alike. As Dr. Bruce Y. Lee, a physician, scientist, researcher, businessman, and computer modeler, told me, "If you really want to tackle the issue of mentorship and improve it, you have to turn it into a science."

Dr. Lee knows a thing or two about tackling issues from a scientific approach. Holding an undergraduate degree from Harvard University, an MD from Harvard Medical School, and an MBA from Stanford Graduate School of Business, his educational pedigree speaks volumes. He is also a health and medicine journalist with over 87 million reads of his *Forbes* articles. And he has been awarded more than $60 million in grants as a principal investigator on health issues. His work has taken him to six continents.

Dr. Lee believes mentorship can be thought of as an emotional concept that can and should be researched systematically because, although the concept of mentorship has been around for centuries, the understanding of mentorship became muddied with the broad application of the term in everyday language and loose definitions. In blogs and media outlets, the word "mentor" is used interchangeably with "coach," "sponsor," "advisor," "counselor," "preceptor," and "instructor." This creates limitations in how we approach mentoring. Without a clear definition of mentorship and a structured approach to its assessment, both individuals and organizations may struggle to achieve consistency in their mentorship endeavors. When a term is used to explain everything, it explains nothing.

Organizations can and often do miss out when they create mentoring programs based on inaccurate information. It is discouraging when these programs fail to yield the expected results. People then lose their belief in the concept when what is really the problem is faulty understanding and application. Similarly, individuals experience loss when their search for meaningful connections doesn't pan out as they had envisioned. Sometimes, the connections they form are superficial and transactional because they believe "a connection is a connection" rather than realizing that connections must be meaningful to succeed. Both organizations and individuals need to approach mentoring with clarity and realistic expectations.

Where Can Research Take Us?

Research can help us define and understand the concept of mentorship. New mentoring terms pop up all the time, such as mutual mentorship and "friendtor." This shows that the understanding of the concept of mentorship needs to be well defined so that we can build our programs on a solid foundation. Research on mentoring will enable us to discuss mentoring in ways that will lead to appropriate engagement and positive outcomes.

We haven't fully grasped the concept of mentorship comprehensively. We need answers to the following questions: What constitutes mentorship? What are the different kinds of mentorship? Who takes on the role of a mentor? What motivates individuals to become mentors? What are the effective and ineffective aspects of mentoring programs? What advantages does mentoring offer from both the mentor's and mentee's perspectives? In what ways does mentorship contribute to the development of individuals, communities, and workplaces? How do we evaluate the outcome of mentoring?

What Research Has Been Done?

There's limited research aimed at defining mentorship, but a team of researchers from the University of Wisconsin-Madison is actively working on creating a universally understandable definition of mentorship in the workplace through peer-reviewed studies. Drs. Christine Pfund, Angela Byars-Winston, and Jenna Rogers, all academic researchers specializing in mentoring, are concentrating on professional mentorship realms, distinct from the broader, everyday-life mentoring definitions. Historically, there have been over 50 definitions of mentoring (Crisp and Cruz 2009). However, recent years have seen a shift toward viewing mentoring as dynamic, collaborative, and reciprocal relationships where both mentor and mentee play active roles (McGee 2016). The National Academies of Science, Engineering, and Medicine provide a definition: "Mentorship is a professional, working alliance in which individuals work together over time to support the personal and professional growth, development, and success of the relational partners through the provision of career and psychosocial support" (Byars-Winston and Dahlberg 2019). While developed primarily for practitioners and researchers, this definition serves as a foundational concept across many disciplines, encompassing various mentoring relationships. The research by Drs. Pfund, Byars-Winston, and Rogers focuses on mentoring in higher education, particularly among undergraduates, graduates, and postgraduates.

The researchers define mentorship in the workplace as a working alliance. They emphasize the mutuality of the relationship, which requires the mentor and mentee to be engaged and benefit from it. Mentorship is a two-way street. Both mentor and mentee are involved and benefit from the relationship.

The bond between the mentor and mentee, creating the working alliance, as based on their research, is the working alliance:

There are three dimensions of the working alliance:

1. Bond: The bond refers to the mentor-mentee relational quality (e.g. regard, trust, rapport).
2. Goal: The goal refers to mutually agreed-upon targeted outcome(s) based on the mentee's developmental need(s).
3. Task: The task relates to perceptions that mentoring techniques or interventions will help achieve the desired goal(s).

The research on mentorship conducted by Drs. Pfund, Byars-Winston, and Rogers focused on mentoring relationships in higher education (undergraduate, graduate, and postgraduate mentees). Dr. Byars-Winston has specifically studied historically underrepresented groups in the science fields to provide a common framework and language for all the components and attributes of mentoring relationships (Byars-Winston et al. 2016). The limitations of this research is that they studied a limited sample of university students. More research is needed looking at larger age groups and work settings. However, their research is setting the stage for defining mentorship in work settings.

Why Is More Research Needed?

There's a critical need for extensive research to grasp mentorship across diverse contexts comprehensively: spanning age groups, developmental stages, hierarchical and lateral structures, and both professional and social environments. Current research on mentorship tends to be narrow, often concentrating on specific age groups or settings. It's crucial to delve into the similarities and differences across these contexts to unlock the full potential of mentorship and expand its benefits to a broader range of settings. By understanding these nuances, we can optimize mentorship's impact and accessibility, fostering growth and support across various domains.

When The Mentor Project was founded, the goal was to form a research group that could define mentoring and mentoring concepts based on the academic research that was already completed. This was because there was so much noise. New definitions had popped up in the mainstream media, and businesses and colleges were forming mentoring programs based on intuition rather than research. It took nearly four years for us to get our research team in place at The Mentor Project. Our first goal was to tackle the research that has already been done and lay the foundation that is needed to address the much-needed further research on mentorship. When The Mentor Project formed our research group, knowing many studies would be needed in order to understand questions ranging from the practice of mentoring (what motivates mentors to serve as mentors) and what are the benefits of mentoring for the mentors, and what do mentors recommend for mentoring programs. We thought it important to learn more about what research studies from multiple disciplines, ages, and program types could tell us if we were able to look at them as a whole. We found that much more research is needed. We also found that much of the research has a narrow focus and is hard to generalize to a larger population. Our work will be the beginning of a broad look at mentorship and will combine the work of many to help generalize findings to the larger population. We are just beginning the process.

Why Start with a Systematic Review

A systematic review lays the foundation for understanding a concept. It provides a broad overview by looking at all of the research that has been done on a topic. Think of it as similar to the first part of a movie, where you can see the plot being laid out. A systematic review provides us with an understanding of what has been done, whether there is any new information we need to add to that understanding, and how that information can be applied to what we know. It uses detailed, established, scientifically valid methods to look at all of the different studies that have been conducted.

Understanding the science of a concept such as mentorship via a systematic review is the first step to get the lay of the land by determining:

1. What is known,
2. Whether there are gaps in the evidence supplied by the currently available research studies; and
3. How can this knowledge be applied.

It was my great fortune to find a researcher who also wanted to mentor. Dr. Jennifer Wisdom is a clinical psychologist who also serves as director of research for The Mentor Project. She joined our organization because she wanted an opportunity to mentor students in research. Many students think of research as boring and difficult. Jennifer reacts differently. Her face lights up, and she becomes animated when she talks about research. Jennifer wanted to show students that research is an opportunity to explore areas that excite them and can be applied to learn about any topic of interest.

Without delay, two high school students eagerly joined her research group: Jacob Greene from the United States and Sarah Domsky from Mexico. Our program administrator, Samantha Stone, and I also joined. Dr. Wisdom added an associate director, Dr. Cynthia Morrow, and we were set. We met weekly over Zoom. What unfolded was a revelation: Dr. Wisdom's diverse background and wealth of expertise became a beacon of inspiration each week. Our group was simultaneously mentoring laterally and hierarchically, with Jennifer and Cynthia mentoring me laterally (I never learned systematic review in graduate school), and both Jennifer and Cynthia hierarchically mentored Samantha, Jacob, and Sarah. I have experience with research, so I was learning one new component from my peers, to add to my research knowledge. Samantha, Jacob, and Sarah did not have any experience with research. They were novices being guided by experts.

Jennifer's road to research was not direct and makes for an interesting perspective. Right out of high school, she joined the Army to train to become a photojournalist. She did her regular training alongside the enlisted soldiers and then went to advanced individual training at the Defense Information School in Indianapolis (which has since moved to Maryland) for journalism. The Defense Information School is a premier Department of Defense program with distinguished graduates, including Al Gore, Dan Quayle, Gene Siskel, and Walter Mondale.

In 1990, just before the onset of the first Gulf War, Jennifer embarked on her basic training and unexpectedly found herself in a war zone. Her assignment was with the air defense, and she rotated between Saudi Arabia and Bahrain, closely working alongside soldiers. Following this intense experience, she returned to the Defense Information School, where she delved into intermediate photojournalism and editing courses. Soon after, she was dispatched to the National Training Center, a desert warfare training facility located in California. Here, Jennifer assumed the role of an in-house journalist for the Army, diligently crafting articles that always involved an element of research.

Upon completing her service in the Army, she switched gears and embarked on a journey toward a doctoral degree in clinical psychology at George Washington University in Washington, DC. She views mentorship from the perspective of the concepts it embodies (the words we use), the organization required to make it work, and the entire field. She zooms out, looking at the big picture, then zooms in to look at the individual, and then zooms out again to the general population that the mentoring is about. This zooming in and out is a way of connecting any disconnects—if you only see the population or only see the person, there is a disconnect.

Jennifer has had years of education and special training in journalism and editing and doctoral-level training in statistics. These are very advanced skills that require years to master. So when she proposed we work with high school students to teach them how to do systematic reviews and then teach them how to write peer-reviewed journal articles, I wondered whether this was a realistic endeavor. I asked, "Would the students be able to follow the concepts?" Jennifer was confident, however. She answered, "I'm not sure why high school students haven't already been doing it. Young people are like sponges, especially high school students ready to absorb stuff left and right." She explained that I should think of it like Bloom's taxonomy versus just looking at information. Bloom's taxonomy classifies learning objectives for students with three learning domains: cognitive, affective, and psychomotor. What that really boils down to is how we think, how we feel, and how we move. Jennifer was just transposing Bloom to mental processes. The way she saw it, she wasn't just teaching students information, she was teaching them how to think about information.

We decided to move forward with a systematic review of existing research to take a comprehensive look at mentorship. She did not want to limit the work to looking at a narrow aspect of it; she wanted a broad overview as well. She argued that we can always narrow the focus if we can see trends and overarching themes. Having a broad view allows us to figure out whether there is an aspect of mentorship that hasn't been studied or whether we have a rich set of data in an area of mentorship that no one has tapped into yet. Our goal was to answer questions about mentoring and fill in gaps in the research. We would also examine the anecdotal myths, accepting those that proved valid and debunking those that did not. In this way, it would lay the foundation for future work in mentoring.

Define, Combine, and Apply

The overarching goal of our research was to define the concept of mentorship and understand how it is practiced. We needed to combine all of the findings from the studies to see where they overlapped and where there were gaps. Finally, we needed to be able to write, speak, and create programs based on the research so we aren't reinventing the wheel or forming new programs based on anecdotes.

As mentioned, I, like many people, didn't learn this form of research in graduate school. The value to the students on our team is tremendous (and to me as well!). We started with a whopping 303,000 abstracts and whittled them down to more than 3,000 papers to review. Reading through hundreds of abstracts (short summaries of the articles) helped us begin to see how people in education, medical schools, nursing programs, and other disciplines were talking about and defining mentoring. There are different perspectives in each, and the goals for each were different.

Our research had specific learning objectives. The valuable knowledge gained during the systematic review will not only benefit future research endeavors but will also enhance our ability to navigate and comprehend scholarly articles. The skills developed extend far beyond the scope of this project.

The Learning Breakdown:

1. Learn about mentoring.
2. Learn how to become precise with language.
3. Learn how to analyze a study's methodology—is it an empirical study (e.g. a randomized control study), an editorial, a commentary, etc.?
   (a) If research, was it qualitative or quantitative?
4. What do the data mean?
5. Extract the data and enter it into an Excel spreadsheet.
6. Summarize the results for several different research questions.
7. Learn how to write peer-reviewed articles and submit them.

Jennifer guided her mentees through each step, set up weekly Zoom meetings to go over progress, and worked as a group to review difficult concepts. After a while, the mentees started coming in with their own ideas, clearly progressing in their learning. This was the most gratifying part of the work.

It wasn't unbelievable to Jennifer to think that high school students would read through more than 400 abstracts and then gradually understand the different components of research—not just definitions, but how it all works in real life. Neither student dropped out. Neither student gave up. As I write this, they are still working on this research, nearly one year after they started. The principles of this research are the foundation for other areas of research as well and will help speed the learning process for other projects they may engage in later.

The added bonus with this research are the papers. We didn't know if the mentees would stick it out to the end, or whether they would want to work on writing papers. Throughout, Jennifer gave them an "out" and said they could stop at any time. But they kept working, and they are now excitedly writing the papers with Jennifer and Cynthia. It is beautiful. The world is gaining new knowledge, and this group is moving the needle forward in mentoring research and literature.

Where We Stand Currently

We're exploring various facets of mentorship, delving into what motivates individuals to mentor; common mentoring activities; outcomes of mentoring; barriers faced by mentors, mentees, and mentoring programs; as well as perspectives, benefits, and challenges for mentors; and ways to enhance mentoring experiences. What we're uncovering is a lack of specificity in defining and identifying the core components of mentorship. Studies often portray mentoring in a hierarchical manner, neglecting the importance of lateral mentorship. This needs to be addressed, and we are doing so.

Beyond specificity, there's a pressing need to view mentorship comprehensively, understanding that our daily interactions are intricate and multifaceted. Mentoring can take many forms. From advice, guidance, and support, to specific, timed mentoring sessions, mentoring doesn't always present in the same way. This can make it difficult to report on generally. A university setting may look different from a nursing mentoring program, which may look different from a peer-to-peer mentoring program for campers and a boss mentoring a newcomer.

Research plays a crucial role in identifying commonalities across various settings, such as nursing schools, community programs, and corporate environments. By synthesizing findings, we can consolidate mentoring concepts and identify key ingredients for successful mentoring relationships or programs. This process enables us to discard ineffective practices and focus on what consistently works across diverse studies, preventing overgeneralizations and outright misconceptions that can skew our understanding of mentorship.

Through systematic reviews, we can uncover shared experiences in mentoring and make informed statements about mentors, mentees, and mentoring dynamics based on a comprehensive analysis of multiple studies. This approach enhances our understanding of mentorship and paves the way for more effective mentoring practices in various contexts.

Research serves as the cornerstone upon which our understanding of mentorship is built. It provides the lens through which we decipher the nuances, identify best practices, and unearth hidden potentials within mentorship dynamics. Just as a mentor guides their mentee with wisdom and insight, research guides us in navigating the complexities of mentorship with clarity and purpose.

Why do we mentor? It's more than a mere transaction; it's a value we hold dear. Mentoring reveals our purpose and motivation—the driving force behind our engagement in these transformative relationships.

The fascinating truth? We're still in the infancy of truly comprehending mentorship. It's not just about the *why*; it's also about the *how*, the *with whom*, and the *what*. Research becomes our compass, guiding us through the intricate nuances of mentorship. It helps us define not only who we mentor but also what we seek to achieve when we step into these roles, and why we invest our time, energy, and wisdom.

But research alone doesn't paint the whole picture. Imagine a world of study without seeing or understanding how these individuals operate in real life. We need to learn from those who have done it—those who have experienced being a mentor and those who have walked the path of a mentee. How does mentoring affects their lives? What are their relationships like?

The upcoming chapter delves into the dynamic landscape of contemporary mentoring practices. In today's rapidly advancing technological era, mentorship has undergone a transformative evolution, incorporating innovative methods to guide and support others. The post-COVID world has accelerated this evolution, pushing us to explore new and modern avenues for mentorship. The next chapter illuminates how mentorship continues to adapt and thrive, showcasing its resilience and relevance in shaping future generations.

9

The Future of Mentoring

Mentoring always has the same underlying principles guiding it. Whether formal or informal, hierarchical, lateral, or peer-to-peer, and whether face-to-face or online, mentoring is guided by the five key components: (1) generativity (the mentor has to want to do it), (2) intrinsic motivation (the mentor and mentee have to want the relationship without external rewards/awards/pay as the major incentive), (3) there needs to be a meaningful connection (it is a two-way street), (4) the mentee needs to trust the mentor and vice versa, and (5) finally, there needs to be a goal. The format may change as we develop new avenues for meeting and connecting with others, but these principles remain. Now is an exciting time for mentoring because people can benefit from people they may never meet in person. Or they may meet but communicate and connect in ways we wouldn't have dreamed of just 20 years ago. The advent of the Internet created new ways of connecting and, therefore, modern forms of mentoring. In this chapter I present two examples of how modern mentoring has developed in the past seven years and why they show that we are just at the beginning of what we can expect to see in the future.

Dorie Clark

Around 2017, I reached out to Dorie Clark, an American author and personal branding expert who has helped many individuals become leaders in their areas of expertise. Dorie has a warm personality that draws you in the minute you meet her. She speaks openly about her vulnerabilities, provides new ways of looking at failures, and makes pivoting to new opportunities seem exciting rather than frightening. As I look back on that conversation, where I dubbed her a modern mentor, I realized this was about the time I was beginning to see a change in how people reached out for guidance and advice from experts. Social media was in full swing, with Facebook, LinkedIn, and Twitter (now X) active spaces for people to connect and share information. Dorie was using social media to sift through the noisy, crowded world of information facing us all. Just as it was getting harder and harder for talented professionals to get their good ideas heard, Dorie was cracking the code. She realized that being able to spread a message required more than just a good idea. People needed to know how to disseminate their message to those who needed and wanted to hear it.

Dorie figured out how to do this online. She wasn't just throwing spaghetti against the wall. She connected with people in person, at conferences, think tanks, and companies. While doing this, she was writing and continuing her connection with those she met online. She didn't just spam people willy-nilly. She made herself available to meet with those who wanted to connect. She offered calendar links to meet online. This was before Zoom and before people did this regularly. It seems completely normal, but it wasn't that way seven years ago. Dorie mentored others to help them become recognized for their talents, skills, and abilities. She made her information available via regular newsletters and online personal meetings. She told me, "One of the big opportunities that social media has presented is that we now live in a world where the gatekeepers have been eliminated. You no longer have to wait for a publisher to agree to put your book out or for an editor to be willing to publish your article. If you have ideas, you want to contribute information and help others. You can share it online, directly reach people, and build a following independently." Dorie was mentoring others to do what she had already discovered. She found that you can create meaningful connections and foster them online. She was generous and generative with her knowledge and didn't limit the access to anything she learned. This fostered trust among those who connected with her.

When I first told Dorie I considered her to be a modern mentor because of her social media and online presence, she didn't quite get it at first. As we continued to talk, she understood and responded, "Social media provides a really powerful forum for providing mentorship from afar and especially if you operate in a specialized niche that may not be appreciated or recognized by the mainstream gatekeepers. You have a direct path to putting out information and having it serve as a beacon that can attract like-minded people who are drawn to your perspective and the information you're sharing."

Social media and online presence have grown exponentially since then, especially since COVID-19. We spend much more of our time online connecting with others, having meetings, exchanging texts, videos, pictures, ideas, skills, and knowledge. There is meaning in how these exchanges happen. Many of us have modern mentors like Dorie, who we didn't realize were mentors because the format was so new. Most people feel connected in a meaningful way with their mentors online. I learn from so many, including Dorie, when I read her newsletters, watch her videos, and see her posts. She and I connected in person, and she also knows my husband, but I'd say most of our communication has been online. When she sends a kind comment about a goal I've met, it means something to me. When I ask her questions, she answers them, and I feel connected with her. She is a modern mentor.

Marshall Goldsmith

Marshall Goldsmith is one of the world's leading executive educators, coaches, and authors. His clientele list boasts over 150 top-tier CEOs. When we spoke, I asked him about his thoughts on modern mentoring. How has mentoring changed, and where is it going? Marshall answered that it revolves around leveraging technology to facilitate mentorship in new and innovative ways. He believes that while mentoring principles remain the same, technological advancements have enabled novel approaches to mentorship. When I asked him about the most recent revolutionary technological change, he mentioned the addition of AI.

The evolution of his own efforts in mentoring, held back in the past due to technological limitations, finally hit with the advent of new AI technology. He created "The Marshall Bot," an AI-generated bot that serves as a mentorship tool, providing advice and insights based on his expertise. Marshall is making all his knowledge accessible to anyone for free via a chatbot that has been extensively fed with his stories and experiences. Like other AI-generated tools, such as ChatGPT and Bing, the Marshall Bot learns from everything it takes in and from all of the "conversations" it has with those using it. More than $1 million was used to create and update this bot. It is checked repeatedly for accuracy and has all of its responses monitored so that it responds as if Marshall himself were answering.

I tried it and found that I could use this new bot; it provided stories to illustrate concepts and to help provide context for questions I asked. There is also a prototype in the works, due out by the end of 2024, which has Marshall speaking, and you really cannot tell that it is not him speaking in person. The bot has such an expansive understanding that Marshall describes instances where the bot's responses have prompted him to make connections between concepts that he hadn't previously considered. Moreover, Marshall values the personalized nature of the Marshall bot, which offers a more authentic and humanlike interaction compared to other AI-driven platforms. He appreciates that the bot reflects his opinions and perspectives rather than providing generic or consensus-based responses.

This form of modern mentoring is dynamic and enriching. It benefits the mentor by having their legacy put out into the world; it benefits the mentee by enhancing communication in a nurturing environment. It can interact with more people than any one individual, and it can go on when the person is no longer around. It represents a true legacy. And it does all of this without losing the "personal touch." The feeling of connection exists in the person-to-AI conversations. It feels natural and supportive. Mentorship becomes available to anyone around the world. Marshall commands roughly $50,000 per speaking engagement. He is not personally accessible financially and geographically to most people worldwide. With this new form of modern mentoring, he can be everywhere and available to everyone anytime. Imagine being mentored by someone you've always looked to for advice but likely would never have an opportunity to meet in person (including online). The impact of this is tremendous. The value to those who take advantage of modern mentorship is that they can quickly absorb new concepts and knowledge. Gone are the days of scheduling a meeting months in advance. If you have a question, a response is available instantly. Hello to a future full of mentoring potential!

Mentoring by Video

Mentoring can include providing videos. From YouTube to Tik-Tok to online libraries, modern mentoring can include access to information that isn't direct between the mentor and mentee. For example, a mentor can meet with a mentee, and resources can be available online to help guide a person to a higher level in reaching their goal. This is common now. The Mentor Project has more than 400 online video resources for mentees to access. They are created by and provided by the mentors to help with the mentoring process. For example, mentees who are looking to innovate may want information on what it means to copyright and when you need to trademark something. A mentee doesn't need to contact the mentor for this. The mentee can watch a video, move themselves along in their goal, and access the mentor as needed for guidance. This modern support helps streamline the mentoring process. AI bots are available now to support efforts in many fields, which can help further bond a mentor and mentee. A mentee can move along their goal trajectory at their own pace whether as a support or as a main component of mentoring. Video and online resources are becoming a big part of modern mentoring.

The examples of Dorie, Marshall, and videos are the beginning of a new form of mentoring, just like social media and the Internet, which opened doors and removed gatekeepers, who might limit access to information. With the advent of mentoring bots, we will have many more opportunities to access guidance and advice. Modern mentoring is in its infancy, and no one knows what the future will provide. One thing we can be sure of is that mentoring will be easier to access globally, with our experts becoming more and more available to everyone.

The way we can look at modern mentoring is to look for opportunities to infuse the five key components into any form of online, video, or AI connection we make. We don't need to be in a face-to-face connection to feel connected. Think of long-distance relationships with family, friends, and loved ones. We don't lose the feeling of connection when these others are far away. The same is the case with modern mentoring. To create a strong modern mentoring relationship, infuse as many of the five key components into the relationship as possible. Becoming aware of what goes into a solid mentoring relationship will help strengthen all forms of mentoring we engage in.

The idea of adding AI to relationships may seem scary. Where is the personal interaction, and are we losing our humanity? I think this change is similar to when we started to use telehealth when treating individuals with medical and mental health treatments. It was frowned upon in the beginning, but we really saw how useful this mode of treatment is when COVID hit. AI should not be thought of as a replacement for mentorship, but it should be considered an adjunct to mentorship. It is also an opportunity to keep the library of our most precious natural resources—our experts—alive and their knowledge, skills, and values retained. I see AI as a way of preserving our library of expertise from mentors that would otherwise be at risk of being lost if it weren't for the AI opportunity and modern mentoring approaches we are seeing now.

Mentoring has long been thought of as hierarchical. A one-to-one relationship between a mentor and a mentee, like an apprenticeship. The future of mentoring is a shift in seeing mentorship as strictly hierarchical, and instead, seeing it as multidirectional. In recent years, other forms of mentoring have been described, such as peer mentoring, bringing two peers together (often in a school setting), with one peer teaching the other a concept. An example of this was given in Chapter 5, when a fellow graduate student called me at work in a panic, asking me to help her with a statistics calculation. We organically connected because my classmate knew I would want to help her and would do so without asking or wanting anything in return. She trusted me, knew me well, and had an immediate goal. The five key components of mentoring still apply. I refer to this kind of mentoring as lateral mentoring™, a term I coined about eight years ago. It describes mentoring relationships with experts who are not above us, who guide and mentor us. This is generally organic, rather than through matching, is informal, and very powerful in its impact. This can happen anywhere (for example, in the workplace or in leisure activities). Peer mentoring, on the other hand, is usually a formal mentoring relationship and often involves matching. Like a dating app, a mentor is matched with a mentee based on skill sets and work commonalities. The future of mentorship will include the acknowledgment of lateral mentoring™ in personal and work settings. Mentorship is evolving. New ways of giving and receiving mentorship are becoming available to us rapidly.

As we transition from exploring the future of mentoring and its limitless potential, a compelling narrative emerges, highlighting the profound impact of mentoring on culture. Mentorship is not just about sharing knowledge and guidance; it is about nurturing connections and facilitating growth on a broader scale. This transition urges us to recognize the transformative role of mentorship in shaping cultures in family, friendship, communities, and the workplace. The next chapter emphasizes the ripple effects of even small mentorship acts, calling us to embrace mentoring relationships and contribute to a collective culture of learning, development, and empowerment.

10 Creating Culture through Mentorship

Mentorship transcends individual interactions; it embodies an exchange of meaning, passion, and motivation. Mentorship takes expertise honed by one person and passes it on to another, often expanding its impact. This dynamic process isn't confined to personal growth; it permeates and shapes cultures as well. Whether in our communities, workplaces, families, or friendships, mentorship catalyzes change, propelling us toward new horizons and collective growth.

According to Hazel Markus, culture motivates people to action (Markus 2016). For most, this motivation stems from openness to certain individuals, meeting expectations, and adhering to cultural norms. Motivation is shaped by culture. Cultures encompass sets of ideas, interactions, and institutions that influence individuals' behaviors. This is important because the culture embodied in each of the many aspects of our life (e.g. work, family, friends) has different meaning and can influence our behavior in different ways. Mentorship helps create culture in all of the areas of our life, and the ways in which we interact with others can affect our cultures.

The Birth of a Nation

An enormously important and far-reaching cultural change due to mentoring occurred when our Founding Fathers, united in purpose and vision, engaged in lateral mentorship™. Drawing upon their diverse skills and expertise, they collaborated to forge a new nation, shedding their colonial identity to establish a new, independent, and distinct culture. Through lateral mentoring™, they navigated uncharted territories, crafting innovative laws, shaping a fresh perception of governance, and igniting revolutionary ideas that fueled the birth of a nation. This transformative act of mentorship wasn't merely a political shift; it was a profound cultural metamorphosis, marking the dawn of a new era defined by self-determination, resilience, and collective aspiration.

The Founding Fathers contributed their ideas, leadership, and efforts to establish the United States as an independent nation. To do this, they had to create and then modify its early political institutions. They were a group of leaders with diverse skills from the 13 American colonies who came together during the late 18th century to challenge British colonial rule and establish a new nation. They drafted the Declaration of Independence in 1776, declaring the colonies' independence from British rule. This pivotal moment gave meaning and purpose to the American Revolutionary War and led to the formation of the United States of America. The Founding Fathers, including notable figures such as George Washington, Thomas Jefferson, John Adams, Benjamin Franklin, James Madison, Alexander Hamilton, and John Jay, played crucial roles in shaping the country's early political structures by drafting the Constitution, thereby laying the foundation for an entirely new form of government. A new culture emerged from this group of lateral mentors™: a representative democratic governance in the new nation.

Without the diverse expertise from this talented group of lateral mentors™ (which included statesmen, diplomats, military leaders, writers, innovators, and thinkers) coming together and combining their unique skills, this new way of thinking about our country could not have come about. They made significant contributions to the success of the American Revolution by drafting the Declaration of Independence, the United States Constitution, and other foundational documents, and even created a new and innovative banking system. They created a whole new culture and a new way of governing a new nation. The world changed with the birth of the United States of America.

The Technology Boom

The 1970s saw the beginning of the technology boom, which is still ongoing. Several key developments laid the groundwork for rapid technological advancements that moved us from the golden yellow wall phone, encyclopedias, TV dinners cooked in the oven, typewriters, televisions with only four major channels, record players, pay phones, and phone books to a world with cell phones, personal computers, microwave ovens, the Internet, streaming television and music, and video games. Our culture changed swiftly. In just one generation, our world became much smaller. The ultimate result was that, as Thomas Friedman put it, the world became flat (Friedman 2005). We communicate with people around the world using video calls. Business meetings are held online. Families can communicate regularly on FaceTime and Zoom from anywhere in the world. We are more globally connected than we've ever been before. News is instant. We know what is happening around the world at any given time because of technological advances. We now have a true world economy. These advances did not occur in a silo. They happened because of lateral mentoring™.

Take personal computing as an example. The Apple Computer was developed by Steve Jobs and Steve Wozniak. They each contributed different skill sets to this endeavor. Steve Jobs was a marketing genius, and Steve Wozniak was an engineering genius. They could not have formed Apple without one another. The world changed and our culture changed when Apple was formed. Steve and Steve were lateral mentors™ long before Apple Computer, and their mentoring relationship led them to usher in an incredible global culture change when the Apple Computer hit the market in 1976, followed by IBM in 1981. Suddenly the average person had access to a personal computer at work and at home. Typewriters became a thing of the past, and this was just the beginning. The culture change was just getting started.

Decade after decade, even year after year, new technological innovation emerged. The 1980s saw significant advancements in software development. By 1989, the world wide web had made its debut. The 1990s saw the dot-com boom (and bust) and the expansion of the Internet. The 2000s witnessed the rise of mobile technology and social media. Our culture changed in what seems like a blink of an eye for those of us who grew up in the 1980s. One day we were talking on phones connected to the walls in our homes, doing our homework from encyclopedias, getting up from the couch to change the channel on the television, and listening to the radio from enormous devices with huge speakers, to having all of those devices wrapped into one tiny device (the cell phone) that we carry in our pocket. Mentoring powerfully contributed to this culture change.

Workplace Culture

When we are at work, we don't often think of changing the culture of the workplace through mentoring. We think, instead, of how mentoring can help us. Just us, one person. But that's just the tip of the iceberg. Mentorship can and does often change the entire culture of the workplace. Work culture is something that is passed on from one person to another. Mentoring doesn't just pass on a skill; it also passes on values and culture.

Years ago, I worked in a large institution with a work culture that included smiling and saying hello to everyone you passed in the hallway, or anywhere, for that matter. That small gesture, which was communicated to me by my boss when I started, permeated beyond the passing gesture. It created a warmth that seeped into everything else. The environment was friendly and, if someone didn't fall in line with this culture, they were considered to be weird, or potentially problematic. They weren't fully trusted. This culture didn't evolve from a human resources handbook. It came from my boss, who was also my mentor, passing this information on to me. It came from others passing it on as well, and, in turn, I communicated it to every new hire under me. I passed it on.

We all see various forms of culture in the workplace. Take coming in early, or staying late. How often has someone stayed late because that was the culture in the workplace? Was leaving at 5 p.m. seen as a negative? There are many aspects of work that are culture driven, and most come from one person passing this on to another. One mentor to another, often informally, until it becomes a cultural norm.

Collegiality is often mentor-based. When mentorship is promoted in the workplace, with individuals seeking and giving guidance and advice in meaningful ways to colleagues, we see a friendly workplace. Employees work better and harder when they trust their colleagues and are able to express vulnerability. Organizations such as Bell Labs thrived on lateral mentorship, and colleagues were happy to help each other, as Bill Cheswick explained in Chapter 4. Culture in the workplace is affected by mentorship because meaningful connections form, creating a friendlier environment.

Organizations that neglect to foster a culture of mentorship may face significant challenges that can impact their overall success and effectiveness. Take Boeing, for instance. The company's well-documented issues with workplace culture, safety concerns, and leadership controversies not only tarnished its reputation but also highlighted deeper-rooted problems within its organization. Without a strong mentorship culture, employees may feel isolated and lack the guidance needed to navigate complex challenges and make informed decisions.

Boeing faced a major crisis in 2018 when Lion Air Flight 610, flying a 737 Max, crashed shortly after takeoff, resulting in the loss of all passengers and crew. The crashes involving the Boeing 737 Max, specifically Lion Air Flight 610 in October 2018 and Ethiopian Airlines Flight 302 in March 2019, were primarily attributed to issues with the aircraft's flight control system. Faulty sensor data and software issues caused the pilots to lose control of the plane, which led to a rapid descent, ultimately resulting in crashes shortly after takeoff.

These issues prompted regulatory authorities worldwide to ground the Boeing 737 Max fleet until safety modifications and additional training requirements were implemented to address the concerns raised by the crashes.

Boeing has continued to grapple with the fallout from these crises as well as COVID-19-related production slowdowns, layoffs, and financial challenges. As Boeing's internal practices unfolded through media coverage, congressional hearings, regulatory reports, and statements from whistleblowers, the public became more aware of whistleblower issues and allegations of retaliation. These revelations contributed to the ongoing scrutiny of Boeing's corporate culture, safety protocols, regulatory compliance, and accountability mechanisms.

Although mentorship may not have been explicitly highlighted or discussed extensively in public statements or reports about Boeing's work culture, its potential impact on leadership, safety, and employee engagement is a topic of interest and scrutiny within broader discussions about the company's challenges and efforts to address organizational issues.

If we look at Boeing as an example of how things can go wrong, the components of the way they operated were directly opposite of what is required in mentoring. Their workplace culture seemed rife with communication breakdown, lack of transparency, and management styles that hindered innovation and collaboration. These are directly opposite of what mentoring offers, i.e. generativity (caring for others), intrinsic motivation, meaningful connections, trust, and goals. Without the bond that mentoring fosters, without the trust and communication, a breakdown in culture can arise and snowball out of control. In this case, that seems to have happened.

Organizations that prioritize mentorship create environments where knowledge sharing, collaboration, and professional development thrive. For example, companies such as Google and Microsoft have robust mentorship programs that empower employees to learn from experienced colleagues, build valuable relationships, and contribute more effectively to the organization's success. As mentioned in Chapter 5, and Colgate-Palmolive also has a mentoring program that adds to a positive work culture. They understand that mentorship is not just about individual growth but also about shaping a positive and inclusive work culture where employees feel supported, valued, and motivated to excel.

Mentorship plays a crucial role in shaping work culture by fostering collaboration, knowledge sharing, ethical behavior, and professional development. Companies that fail to prioritize mentorship risk experiencing issues like those seen at Boeing, whereas those that embrace mentorship create environments where employees thrive and contribute meaningfully to organizational success.

Mentorship Culture within Communities

Communities grow and develop, like a snowball growing in size and speed as it rolls down a mountain, when mentoring is at the core of the culture. An example of a community whose culture has been significantly shaped by mentorship is the Silicon Valley tech community in California. Although tech is now dispersed so that Silicon Valley isn't the hub any longer, mentorship has played a crucial role in the development, innovation, and success of this renowned technology hub.

The culture of Silicon Valley grew out of the regular practice of hierarchical and lateral mentoring™. Knowledge sharing and innovation were key. Established tech leaders and entrepreneurs actively mentored aspiring start-up founders, engineers, and tech enthusiasts. Mentorship facilitated the exchange of ideas, best practices, and technical knowledge, leading to groundbreaking innovations in software development, artificial intelligence, and digital technology.

The culture didn't develop overnight. The groundwork for the tech culture in the region started in the 1940s with the development of semiconductor technology and with companies such as Hewlett-Packard setting up shop near Stanford University. The presence of skilled engineers and scientists was established. The 1960s and 1970s were a time of rapid growth, building upon the foundation set decades earlier. This was the birth of Apple, Xerox, and Intel. The rise of companies settling in the region continued to the present day. Now Silicon Valley has Facebook and Google.

Mentorship has been instrumental in nurturing the entrepreneurial ecosystem in Silicon Valley and has been a part of its culture since the beginning. Experienced mentors provide guidance to early-stage start-ups and aspiring entrepreneurs. This culture encourages risk-taking, resilience, and creativity for new ventures.

Throughout its history, Silicon Valley has been characterized by a unique ecosystem that includes world-class universities, research institutions, venture capital firms, start-up incubators, and a culture of collaboration, risk-taking, and innovation. This ecosystem has attracted top talent, investment capital, and industry leaders, cementing Silicon Valley's reputation as a global epicenter of technology and entrepreneurship.

Mentorship has a key role in career development and individual advancement in the Silicon Valley tech community. The mentorship culture promotes continuous learning, professional growth, and talent retention within the tech industry. Silicon Valley as a community has been known for this and has created a sense of community support and engagement as a result. Mentorship has been a driving force in shaping the culture of innovation, entrepreneurship, and collaboration in the Silicon Valley tech community for more than seven decades.

Families

What was the last holiday you celebrated with family? For most, traditions are passed on from one generation to the next. Whether it is the dishes served on the dinner table or the decorations in the house, families bond over traditions. There is a feeling of comfort when you know what to expect when a holiday arrives and you can anticipate the food and the rituals. Familiarity breeds contentment. Mentorship is the torch passing the traditions, values, and rituals from one generation to the next, creating a culture within the family.

When my husband and I got engaged, we both entered new family cultures. My husband's family culture was all about food and education. If you entered the house, you didn't go to the living room. In fact, we rarely ever went into the living room. We immediately sat in the kitchen. Magically, food would appear. Even if we weren't expected. We caught up with each other over food. When my husband was introduced to my family, I instructed him to eat in advance because he probably wouldn't see a morsel of food for hours after arrival. We'd enter the house and move directly to the living room to sit and converse for hours (without food).

My husband's parents were immigrants who came to the United States seeking all of the privileges many of us take for granted. One was education. Both of his parents had been denied a high school degree and expected their children to achieve the highest level of education possible. They succeeded, because their three children became a physician, a PhD, and a lawyer. In my family, education was not thought much of. I could attend college if I wanted, but no one pressured me. When I got my PhD, my husband's parents threw a post-graduation celebration for me at their house (with tons of food). It didn't occur to my parents. Not that they didn't care—it just wasn't part of their culture.

In both families, these differences in customs, traditions, and values were passed on from previous generations. An example from my grandmother's mentorship of me may illustrate what I mean: "We eat to live. We don't live to eat." This was something she was taught and that she taught my mother. Food was never something we thought about when I was growing up, or when we visited my mother's parents' house. Similarly, my grandmother said to me, "You can marry a rich man just as easily as you can marry a poor man." Education wasn't pushed, because after all, I could always marry a rich man. This was a family culture that was passed down from one generation to the next.

Think of your family. What was passed on to you and what are you passing on to the next generation? It might be religious traditions, food, education, a business, or values. All of these create a culture in the family that underlies how a family operates—some more smoothly than others.

Grandparents are often mentors who pass on vital family culture to their grandchildren. My grandfather took me out weekly when running his errands. I learned much from him that I still hold today and am passing on to my children. What might seem like a routine interaction could easily be a passing of vital culture, just like our holiday traditions and meals can carry on for generations (I cook my grandmother's turkey dinner for Thanksgiving from her handwritten recipes every year). Religion is passed on from generation to generation, and the values of the family get passed on as well. This is all through mentorship, and the culture of each family carries at least a part of what has been passed on to them.

Friends and Mentorship

Mentorship can play a significant role in shaping the culture within friendships, fostering mutual growth and support. Friends are prolific lateral mentors™. Think of all of the times you helped a friend solve a problem. How many times have you guided a friend through a new relationship or a breakup? What about advice and guidance for a new job, new house, or car? The mentoring interactions are limitless with friends.

Mentorship can create culture in friendships through learning and growth. Friends mentor each other in areas of expertise or experience, sharing knowledge, skills, and insights to help each other develop personally. My son Liam is a college student, and he shares his mentoring experiences with friends he's made. Most recently, he participated in a fashion show at school as a model. Two students who are friends and professional models mentored him and the other novices in how to walk the runway. He and his friends weren't paid. His professional model friends wanted to help Liam and the others learn to walk the runway, how to do what they do professionally. The two mentors not only taught their mentees about the line of work but also how to do an aspect of it—walking the runway. Liam learned that modeling is more than showing up and walking around in clothes. It required a lot of work. As with any mentoring relationship, this one consisted of accountability, support, empowerment, encouragement, commitment, feedback, and reflection.

Friends create a culture that allows for expressing vulnerabilities and trusting that their friends have their best interest in mind and will guide them to elevate their skills. Learning new skills and performing in front of a crowd of more than 300 people could be frightening, but with mentors guiding him, Liam felt excited. It was a personal growth experience for him. How many times have you experienced mentorship from a friend or group of friends?

We need friends throughout our lives. Friends help us grow and develop, and these lateral mentors™ help us create a friendship culture. Think of the culture you have with your friends. Do you take girls trips? Or guy trips? Do you have special occasions set aside for friends? Do you have a friend group at work or at home? What is the culture? Do you have more than one friend group? Perhaps a fun friend group where you engage in fun events? Or a sports group? I have a pickleball group that has expanded beyond the court—we are going to a gala together this year. The culture of this group is fun and free of any work or home focus. Along the way, we also mentor each other. Rachael has mentored me in hitting my mark with my shots. Irene mentors me in her specialty—the drop shot. Mentorship-based friendships revolve around shared values (like pickleball), goals, and aspirations. Friends mentor each other based on common interests, passions, and ambitions, creating a culture of alignment and collective achievement.

Writing this book was the result of a friend mentoring me. Ali Binazir, a friend for about four years now, was giving a talk about writing books. He's published several and was encouraging a group of friends to write the book they've always wanted to write. I contacted him and asked him to mentor me. He immediately agreed, and we embarked on a weekly meeting to talk about writing. He helped me develop my confidence to not only start my blog on Substack, "The Right Side of 40," but when I was contacted by Wiley with the possibility of writing a book, I had the confidence to say yes! Writing was something I did regularly, but I didn't feel confident about something as big as a book. Ali helped me develop that confidence, as a friend can. His mentorship improved my writing process, and I probably would not have written this book if it weren't for his guidance. We still talk regularly, though not always about writing. Our friendship started before he became my writing mentor, and it continues still. Just as friendships do—lateral mentoring™ is an aspect of the friendship.

Mentorship-based friendships often involve a long-term commitment and investment in the well-being and growth of the other. My dad always used to say, "You want your friends to succeed just as much as you want yourself to succeed because no one wants to be with a group of people who don't want to better themselves." He always encouraged and helped his friends with personal and work goals and instilled in me the importance of creating a culture of personal and professional growth among friends.

Mentorship creates a culture of learning, support, empowerment, and celebration within friendships, enriching the bond and enhancing the overall quality of the relationship. Friends who engage in mentorship-based interactions contribute to each other's personal and professional development, creating a positive and nurturing environment for growth and fulfillment.

Mentorship has a profound impact on shaping cultures within various contexts, from professional environments to communities, family, and friendships. It fosters learning, collaboration, and empowerment, creating a positive ripple effect that extends beyond individual relationships. As we delve deeper into the transformative power of mentorship, it becomes clear that mentorship is not just about personal development but also about cultural change and collective growth. In the upcoming chapter on the call to action for mentorship, we will explore how you can harness the potential of mentorship to drive meaningful change, inspire others, and cultivate thriving communities.

11 Call to Action: Finding Mentorship Opportunities

Who can be mentored? Anyone. So don't count yourself out! At work, whether we're just starting out or at the top of our fields, mentors can help us get on the path forward or keep the momentum going once we are on the path. In our personal lives, whether we are looking to pass on values, culture, or get a passion project going, mentors can help us with legacies and starting meaningful projects. Putting mentorship into action is as simple as:

Identify - to find a mentor

- Look around and ask yourself, "Is there anyone who can help me in any area of my work or in my personal life?" More often than not, there is someone who can help you with an aspect of your job, learn the lay of the land, or help you find new opportunities inside and outside of work (such as awards). Simply being aware of your coworkers, whether above you, below you, or lateral, you will likely be able to identify several people who would make great mentors at the moment or in the future. Likewise, there are so many people in our personal lives we take for granted and don't consider them when we need guidance for our passion projects and personal growth. Just look to your left and look to your right. Your next mentor is likely right next to you!

Identify - to become a mentor

- Look around and ask yourself, "Is there anyone I can help?" Mentoring others makes us feel great and allows us to pass on what matters most to us so we can leave a legacy. Most lateral mentoring™ relationships will involve each person in the relationship as the mentor or mentee at some point. If you find someone you can mentor, offer to help. You're creating a connection that can lead to future mentoring and a meaningful connection. We all need allies at work and guides in our personal lives, and we are surrounded by them!

Once you identify potential mentoring opportunities as mentor and mentee, chances are your passions and career will advance and your expertise will live on in those you mentor.

Assess - to find a mentor

- Once you've identified potential mentors, assess the individuals for their skills, talents, and expertise. It is important to identify who is a potential mentor, but when we assess, we are digging a little deeper. Figure out what their abilities, expertise, and strengths are so that you can (in the moment or at a later date) engage in mentoring.
- Ask yourself, "Where do they have talents that can support my weaknesses?" You are essentially creating your digital Rolodex of skills, talents, and expertise from which you can seek support now or in the future.

Assess - to become a mentor

- Once you've identified potential people to mentor, assess the individuals for their skills, talents, and expertise. And, just as important as understanding the strengths of others, you need to know your own areas of expertise! You don't have to be the best at anything. You only need to be better than someone else. Your expertise may be exactly where they are lacking. Assess their abilities so that you can (in the moment or at a later date) engage in mentoring.

- Ask yourself, "Where do I have talents that can support their weaknesses?" You are essentially creating your digital Rolodex of skills, talents, and expertise that you can offer to support others.

Superconnectors are great at assessing their own skills and the talents of others. Have you ever met someone who seemingly can connect just about anyone? They've mastered assessing individuals. By assessing the talents and skills of others, you can call on them when you are in need or offer your assistance when they are in need.

Create - with a mentor

- Once you've identified and assessed potential mentors, you can create endless opportunities for advancement for yourself. This is particularly useful when working on teams in the workplace or in groups in the community. You can create opportunities with one mentor or a team of mentors that lead to breakthroughs in the workplace, new passion projects, and significant community change. Your mentors help guide you and elevate you to new levels. This is when mentors share award opportunities and breakthroughs for advancement at work and personal development in your personal life.

Create - as a mentor

- Once you've identified and assessed potential people to mentor, you can create endless opportunities for advancement for others, while keeping your expertise alive. Whether helping someone advance at work, bringing your ideas and expertise to life through their work, or making a personal development change in a person you are mentoring, you are infusing a piece of yourself into them, which continues on and is a form of legacy. Every new creation is an extension of yourself.

If you recall the Steve and Steve example from Chapter 5, Steve Jobs *identified* a friend to help him, *assessed* his friend Steve Wozniak's skill set as better than his in the engineering needed to get the job done, and when he called on him for mentorship, they *created* the new video game that put the world of video gaming on the map for Atari. The identify, assess, and create action plan was explosive in its impact!

A few examples of formal and informal places you can find mentoring opportunities in the workplace:

Formal Opportunities

- **Lunches:** It may seem too simple, but some of the greatest mentoring opportunities have come from organized lunches. An example I learned of several years ago came from a retiring district court judge who said to me, "Imagine being a judge and you've never tried a specific kind of case. Who do you ask for help?" This judge said it is so difficult to ask for help as a judge because a judge is supposed to know everything—that is why they are the judge. Seeking mentorship can be seen as a weakness and may end up leading to others losing confidence in your abilities. This judge proposed organized lunches each week that were designed to get all of the judges together. These lunches allowed the judges to sit and ask the person next to them how they handled a case without necessary divulging their vulnerabilities right away. Lunches and other organized gatherings can break down barriers and lead to mentoring opportunities.
- **Retreats:** Similar to lunches, retreats offer an opportunity to learn more about colleagues, in settings where guards are down and organic mentoring can take place.

- **Sports:** Golf has long been a sport used for mentoring. Deals are made and mentoring happens while playing the game. Other sports can also lead to mentoring.
- **Conferences:** Conferences allow individuals to meet others from outside the organization, which can open up new opportunities for lateral mentoring™. Vulnerabilities may not be the same with people who are not competing for job advancement and career opportunities in your own workplace.
- **Networking organizations:** These are great for meeting new individuals from a variety of fields, who can mentor in personal and professional capacities.

Informal Opportunities

- **Chats:** Chat groups are great for identifying and assessing potential mentors and mentees. Whether you create your own chat group or join one that is offered at the workplace, you can tune in as your needs arise and likely find great mentoring opportunities.
- **Listservs:** Listservs are great for passively monitoring mentoring opportunities. You can check your listserv at your convenience and post if you have a question for others.
- **WhatsApp:** Like a listserv but on the phone, WhatsApp (and other apps such as Signal) offers an opportunity to communicate just like a listserv on email but via texts.
- **Slack and Discord:** These apps can be used on a computer, tablet, or phone for communication within your organization or group you belong to.
- **Watercooler:** The watercooler (or any other office gathering spot) is a place for information exchange and informal discussions that can lead to mentoring opportunities.

There are far more examples that could be listed, but hopefully, these lists show that opportunities to find mentorship abound. The first step is to acknowledge that mentoring is everywhere. Seek mentorship in areas that you feel most insecure about and that you might not want to share with a boss or someone higher on the work ladder (or even in your own department). The goal is to access mentoring and offer mentoring in as many places as possible. You can't have too many mentors. The idea of having just one mentor is limiting. Having many mentors leads to a broader and potentially explosive impact.

A few examples of formal and informal places you can find mentoring opportunities in your personal life:

Formal

- **House of worship:** For those who attend regular services and participate in religious activities, mentorship can be found by engaging with community members who exhibit leadership or expertise in your areas of interest. In most cases, a house of worship is a place where communication and sharing with others is welcome, which can make it an environment ripe for identifying mentors and mentees.
- **Sports:** Join a sports team or club and interact with coaches and players who can provide guidance and mentorship in their area of expertise. Camaraderie is found on sports teams that extends beyond the team, which can lead to mentorship.
- **Social clubs:** Become a member of a social club related to your interests (e.g. book club, hobby group) and connect with experienced members who can mentor you.
- **Community organizations:** Volunteer or join local organizations focused on causes you care about. Engage with leaders and active members who can serve as mentors.

Informal

- **Family and friends:** Seek advice and guidance from family members or friends who have experience and expertise in areas you're interested in.
- **Kids sports/activities and school functions:** Attend events related to your children's activities or school functions and

connect with parents, coaches, or teachers who can offer mentorship.

- **Recreational activities:** Participate in recreational activities such as hiking groups, art classes, or community workshops. Connect with experienced participants who can mentor you.
- **Social media:** Join online communities or groups related to your interests or industry. Engage with experienced members who can provide virtual mentorship.

Each of these settings offers opportunities to build relationships with mentors who can support your personal and professional growth. Once you start identifying potential mentors who are in your everyday life, you'll start to assess and create new mentoring opportunities more often. Mentors are everywhere. Potential mentees are everywhere. We simply need to be aware of them!

Take Action!

Simple Acts Lead to High Impact

- Connect your work with your personal goals. Just look at any entrepreneur who follows a personal passion and turns it into a career. They never do it alone. Mentors are always around guiding.
- Create opportunities for people to connect. Throw a dinner party. Connect others. Create a group chat at work. The key is to connect people. Be the center of the intricate web of individuals who are all interconnected. They are all potential mentors.
- Create opportunities for intrinsic motivation. Remove the extrinsic pay, praise, and rewards from what motivates you and others to get something done. If it requires extrinsic motivation, it isn't going to work well. Look for projects and personal goals that you are motivated to work on or complete without any compensation. If you are a boss, create goals that

align with your employees. This creates room for intrinsic motivation.

- Recognize and celebrate mentoring. Don't take it for granted. Thank your mentors!

Successful mentoring cultivates a thriving team culture, whether in professional settings or personal circles. Building an environment filled with genuine connections inspires everyone to support each other's success. Have you experienced the thrill of being part of a team where every victory is celebrated? Imagine the excitement when a teammate hits a home run, igniting cheers from the entire group. Similarly, when a colleague receives recognition for their outstanding presentation, the collective sense of achievement transcends both work and home spheres. This positive team culture is often a direct outcome of effective mentorship. Colleagues and personal connections who genuinely care about each other naturally strive to lend a helping hand. Trust and camaraderie blossom, fueling collaborative goals that transform into tangible accomplishments.

Having answered the call to action, you are now poised to embark on a journey of transformation through mentorship. As you identify, assess, and create mentorship in your life, you will witness its profound impact not only on your personal growth but also on the broader community, workplace dynamics, and even global initiatives. Mentorship isn't just a practice; it's a catalyst for cultural change. When embraced effectively, it has the power to spark a movement that binds us closer together, fulfilling our aspirations and essential needs.

In closing this book, we have journeyed through the multifaceted world of mentorship. From exploring its deep roots in generativity to the diverse styles that shape mentoring relationships and dispelling misconceptions about what mentoring truly entails, we've explored the motivations that drive us to mentor, uncovering the profound impact it has on us, the organizations we are employed by and that we are engaged with, and society at large. In both professional environments and research settings, we've observed how mentorship nurtures development, sparks creativity, and builds resilience, molding cultures and propelling beneficial transformations.

The role of mentorship is crucial in creating inclusive, supportive environments where learning thrives and potential is realized. We've seen how mentoring transcends boundaries, connecting individuals across generations and backgrounds and fostering a culture of stability, collaboration, empathy, and continuous improvement.

As we conclude, the call to action resounds louder than ever. Let us embrace mentorship as a catalyst for transformation, recognizing its power to inspire, guide, and empower. Committing to nurturing a culture of mentorship, we transform every interaction into a chance for growth, connection, and mutual achievement. Let's unite in a mission of perpetual growth, mentorship, and shared influence, sculpting a radiant tomorrow for all future generations.

References

Ancestry Corporate. n.d. "Company Facts." https://www.ancestry.com/corpo rate/about-ancestry/company-facts.

Byars-Winston, A., and Dahlberg, M. L., eds. 2019. *The Science of Effective Mentorship in STEMM, Online Guide* (Washington, DC: National Academies Press).

Byars-Winston, A., Rogers, J., Branchaw, J., Pribbenow, C., Hanke, R., and Pfund, C. 2016. "New Measures Assessing Predictors of Academic Persistence for Historically Underrepresented Racial/Ethnic Undergraduates in Science." *CBE—Life Sciences Education* 15, no. 3 (2016): ar32.

Crisp G., and Cruz, I. 2009. "Mentoring College Students: A Critical Review of the Literature Between 1990 and 2007." *Research in Higher Education* 50, no. 6 (2009): 525–545. https://doi.org/10.1007/s11162-009-9130-2.

Dixon, S. J. 2024a. "Number of Instagram Users Worldwide from 2019 to 2028." Statista, January 30, 2024. https://www.statista.com/forecasts/1138856/instagram-users-in-the-world.

Dixon, S. J. 2024b. "Facebook: Quarterly Number of MAU (Monthly Active Users) Worldwide 2008–2023." Statista, April 26, 2024. https://www.statista.com/statistics/264810/number-of-monthly-active-facebook-users-worldwide.

Eby, L. T., et al. 2015. "'Cross-lagged Relations between Mentoring Received from Supervisors and Employee OCBs: Disentangling Causal Direction and Identifying Boundary Conditions': Correction to Eby et al. (2015)." *Journal of Applied Psychology* 100, no. 4 (2015): 1318. https://doi.org/10.1037/a0038977.

Erikson, E. H. 1993. *Childhood and Society* (New York: W. W. Norton & Company), 266–267.

Flett G. L., and Marnin J. Heisel, M. J. 2020. "Aging and Feeling Valued Versus Expendable During the COVID-19 Pandemic and Beyond: A Review and Commentary of Why Mattering Is Fundamental to the Health and Well-Being of Older Adults." *International Journal of Mental Health and Addiction* 19, no. 6 (2020): 2443–2469. https://doi.org/10.1007/s11469-020-00339-4.

Friedman, T. L. 2005. *The World Is Flat: A Brief History of the Twenty-first Century* (New York: Farrar, Straus, and Giroux).

Fuligni, A. J., Smola, X. A., and Salek, S. A. 2021. "Feeling Needed and Useful During the Transition to Young Adulthood." *Journal of Research on Adolescence* 32, no. 3 (2021): 1259–1266. https://doi.org/10.1111/jora.12680.

Horowitz B. 2023. "How HR Professionals Can Leave a Powerful Legacy." SHRM HR News. May 2023.

Iqbal, M. 2024. "LinkedIn Usage and Revenue Statistics (2024)." Business of Apps, April 18, 2024. https://www.businessofapps.com/data/linkedin-statistics.

Lefkowitz, R. J. 2018. "A Serendipitous Scientist." *Annual Review of Pharmacology and Toxicology* 58, no. 1 (2018): 17–32. https://doi.org/10.1146/annurev-pharmtox-010617-053149.

Lepper M. R., and Greene, D. 1975. "Turning Play into Work: Effects of Adult Surveillance and Extrinsic Rewards on Children's Intrinsic Motivation." *Journal of Personality and Social Psychology* 31, no. 3 (1975): 479–486. https://doi.org/10.1037/h0076484.

Markus, H. 2016. "What Moves People to Action? Culture and Motivation." *Current Opinion in Psychology* 8 (2016): 161–166.

McGee, R. 2016. "Biomedical Workforce Diversity: The Context for Mentoring to Develop Talents and Foster Success Within the 'Pipeline.'" *AIDS and Behavior* 20, no. S2 (2016): 231–237. https://doi.org/10.1007/s10461-016-1486-7.

Post, S., and Neimark, J. 2007. *Why Good Things Happen to Good People: How to Live a Longer, Healthier, Happier Life by the Simple Act of Giving* (New York: Crown).

Statista. 2024. "Deloitte—Statistics & Facts," January 10, 2024. https://www.statista.com/topics/2602/deloitte/#editorsPicks.

Van Vliet, D., Persoon, A., Bakker, C., Koopmans, R. T., de Vugt, M. E., Bielderman, A. and Gerritsen, D. L. 2017. "Feeling Useful and Engaged in Daily Life: Exploring the Experiences of People with Young-onset Dementia." *International Psychogeriatrics* 29, no. 11 (2017): 1889–1898. https://doi.org/10.1017/s1041610217001314.

Von Post, H., and Wagman, P. 2017. "What Is Important to Patients in Palliative Care? A Scoping Review of the Patient's Perspective." *Scandinavian Journal of Occupational Therapy* 26, no. 1 (2017): 1–8. https://doi.org/10.1080/11038128.2017.1378715.

Acknowledgments

There are many people I'd like to thank.

Joel Weinberger, for reading every chapter, for your support through writing the book, and for being the best husband!

Liam and Aiden Weinberger, for supporting me always and for being the best kids I could ask for!

My dad, Larry Heiser, for always believing in me and for helping me with every project I've ever worked on. You made all of them fun!

Brian Neill for believing in the book, and Julie Kerr for editing the book.

Ali Binazir for being an amazing writing mentor!

The Mentor Project cofounders: Jura Zibas, Bill Cheswick, Larry Heiser, Irene Yachbes, Gabriel Lewis, and Bob Cousins. Without you this wouldn't have happened. You are all my mentors.

The Mentor Project board of directors: Jen Snow, Quintin McGrath, Brian Martin, Kartik Subramanian, and Megen Schlesinger. You are the frontal lobe of The Mentor Project and make magic happen every year.

Samantha Stone for wrangling mentors like no one else can.

The Mentor Project Advisors: Cher Murphy, Anu George, Anand Raghavan, Michelle Lederman, Peter Samuelson, Damon Gersh, Gabriela Ewachiw, Corey Bearak, Fred Klein, Melissa Ashley, and Jennifer Wade.

The Mentors: Alan Zweibel, Alison Escalante, Andrea Rothman, Andy Lopata, Avidor Rabinovich, Aviva Legatt, Ayse Birsel, Bruce Y. Lee, Busayo Odunlami, Cameron Gibson, Charles Camarda, David

Schiff, Deborah Thomson, Desire Banse, Gerry Riskin, Gibor Basri, Hara Marano, Jacklyn Scott, James Freeman, Jane Curth, Javier Francario, Jeff Jennings, Jeff Jensen, Jennifer Wisdom, Jessica Broitman, Justin Thompson, LaTonya Kilpatrick, Lorette Cheswick, Marco Ciapelli, Marilyn Price, Mark Beal, Mary Hagy, Matthew Griffin, Neil Comins, Neil Kane, Patrick Kelley, Ralph Morrison, Richard Mokuolu, Robin Colucci, Roland Mokuolu, Romain Tohouri, Ruth Gotian, Ryan Prior, Sam Gralnick, Sarina Arcari, Steven Rogelberg, Susan Birne-Stone, Suzie Katz, Temi Odunlami, Todd Wallach, Valerie Fridland, Vanessa Small, Vivan Amin, and Zafra Lerman.

Jim "Biscotti" Moriarty for being one of the very first people to believe in my mentoring ideas, Rachael Gazdick for being my mentor, and Chuck Crook, Jacqueline Weinberger, and Sepi Djavaheri for listening to me endlessly talk about mentoring.

About the Author

Dr. Deborah Heiser is the CEO of The Mentor Project and an applied developmental psychologist. She is a *Psychology Today* contributor, author of *The Right Side of 40* blog, coach, *After 40 Podcast* host, and an adjunct professor in the Psychology Department at SUNY Old Westbury. She is a TEDx speaker, a Marshall Goldsmith 100 Coaches coach, and is among the 2022 Thinkers50 Radar Class. She is married with two sons in college.

Index

Page numbers followed by *f* refer to figures.

A
Abbot, Bob, 101, 102
Academic settings:
  lateral mentoring in, 71–73
  mentors in, 87–94
  peer mentoring in, 82–83
Adams, John, 166
ADAR, 81–82
Adelphi University, 28
Adult development theories, xii–xiii, 15*f*
Les Adventures de Telemargu (*The Adventures of Telemachus*; Fenelon), 45–46
Advising, 28–31
Aging, ix–xiv
AI (artificial intelligence), 121, 160–163
Alcorn, Al, 79–80
Allen, BerthaNel, 99
Anchorman: The Legend of Ron Burgundy (film), 56
Anderson, Jim, 100–102
Anecdotal evidence, on mentoring, 143–144
Annual Review of Pharmacology and Toxicology, 59
Apatow, Judd, 56
Apple, 76–77, 143, 167–168, 172
Apprenticeships, 61, 67, 163
Arlington Road (film), 81
Artificial intelligence (AI), 121, 160–163
Aspire, 81
Assessing opportunities, 180–181
Atari, 79
AT&T, 50

B
Bace, Rebecca "Becky," 98–103
Bellitto, Christopher, 46
Bell Labs, 49, 50, 120, 169

Bellovin, Steven, 50
Berei, Judy, 77–78
Binazir, Ali, 176
Blend, 133–134
Bloom's taxonomy, 150–151
BNI (Business Networking International), 34, 35
Boaz (biblical figure), 47
Boeing, 41, 169–171
Bonds, in working alliances, 146
Breakout (video game), 79
Bredella, Miriam, 83–84, 136–139
Brendolyn, 97–98
Brooklyn Polytechnic High School, 74
Buddhism, 45
Business Networking International (BNI), 34, 35
Byars-Winston, Angela, 146–147

C
Camarda, Charlie, 10, 73–76
Campbell, Bill, 143
Chambers of commerce, 34
Chat groups, 183
Cheswick, Bill, xvi–xviii, 49–52, 120, 169
Chief, 36
Children, mentoring, xvii, 51–52
Children's events, 184–185
Chileon (biblical figure), 46
Christianity, 45
CitiGroup, 133
Civil rights movement, 95–96
Clark, Dorie, 158–159
Classmates, as lateral mentors, 71–73
Coaching, 41–43, 115–116
Colgate-Palmolive, 109–117, 171
Colgate Women's Network, 110–112
Collaboration, 80, 130, 171
Collegiality, 169
Comins, Neil, 10, 91–94

Communities, 171–173
Community organizations, 184
Conferences, 183
Connections, *see* Meaningful connections
Cousins, Bob, xvi–xviii, 52
COVID-19 pandemic:
    changes in mentorship due to, 159
    The Mentor Project during, 52
    pivoting during, xviii–xix
    and telehealth, 162–163
Crook, Charles S., II, 94–96
Crook, Susan, 87–90, 94
Culture:
    of families, 173–174
    within friendships, 174–177
    mentorship culture, *see* Mentorship culture
    start-up culture, 76–78
    workplace culture, 168–171

D
Dangerfield, Rodney, 56
Deci, Edward, 21
Declaration of Independence, 166
Defense Information School, 149
Deloitte, 117–123, 171
Dementia, 49
Depression, ix–x
Digital forms, of mentoring, 25–26
Discord, 183
Dissertations, 29
Domsky, Sarah, 149
Dorian Gray, 13

E
Ebenezer Scrooge, 4, 12
Edelman, 78
Elimelech (biblical figure), 46
Emotional development, xiii, 1–3, 2*f*
Entrepreneurs' Organization (EO), 36
Erikson, Erik, xii, 5, 12, 15*f*, 141
Esteem needs (Maslow's hierarchy of needs), 57
Extrinsic motivation, 21–22, 30, 42

F
Facebook (Meta), 34, 35, 158, 172
Family(-ies):
    culture within, 173–174
    as lateral mentors, 73–76
    mentoring opportunities in, 184
    as mentors, 97–98
Fenelon, Frances, 45–46
Firewalls and Internet Security (Cheswick and
        Bellovin), 50

FOC (Friends of Charlie), 74–76
Fordham University, x
Formal mentoring programs, 135–136
Formal opportunities, for mentoring, 182–184
The 40-Year-Old Virgin (film), 56
Founding Fathers, 76, 166–167
Franken, Al, 56
Franklin, Benjamin, 166
Fridland, Valerie, xix
Friedman, Thomas, 167
Friends:
    culture with, 174–177
    as lateral mentors, 73–76
    mentoring opportunities with, 184
    as mentors, 97–98
Friends of Charlie (FOC), 74–76
Friendtor, 145

G
Garnier, J. P., 41
Generativity, 1–16
    becoming generative, 11–12
    as benefit of aging, xiii
    as component of mentoring, 18–21
    development of, 7–9
    fluctuations in, 14–16
    mentoring as form of, 9–11, 141–142
    roots of, 5–7
    and stagnation, 12–13
Generosity, 6, 6*f*, 7
George Bailey (fictional character), 65
Ghamsari, Nima, 133–134
Giving:
    benefits of, 3–4, 6
    as central principle of various religions, 45
Glaxo SmithKline, 41
Goals, in working alliances, 146
Goal setting, 25–26, 142
Goldsmith, Marshall, 4–5, 10, 41–42,
        160–161
Google, 171, 172
Gore, Al, 149
Gotham City Networking, 37, 81
Gotian, Ruth, xix
Grandparents, 94–96, 174
Grassley, Chuck, 32
Gravitation (Misner), 91
Green, Grace, 87–88
Greene, Jacob, 149

H
Hamas, 80
Hamilton, Alexander, 166

Happiness, 2
Harvard Medical School, 137
Harvey Specter (fictional character), 12–13
Health care, 136–139
Heiser, Larry, xviii, 52
Hester, General, 126–127
Hewlett-Packard, 172
Hierarchical mentoring, 67–69
    lateral mentoring vs., 71
    reverse mentoring as form of, 69–70
    in Silicon Valley, 172
Hierarchy of needs (Maslow), 56–57
Hinduism, 45
Homer, 17, 45
HR News, 58
100 Coaches™, 5

I
Identifying opportunities, 179–180
Identity, after retirement, 14
Informal networks, 115
Informal opportunities, for mentoring,
    183–185
Information Security Magazine, 98
Innovation Lab (The Mentor Project), 106
Instagram, 35
Intel, 172
International Design Award, 107
Internet Mapping Project, 50
Internships, 68
Intrinsic motivation, 9, 21–22, 57, 142
Intuit, 143
Islam, 45
Israel, 80–81
It's a Wonderful Life (film), 65

J
Jay, John, 166
Jefferson, Thomas, 166
Jobs, Steve, 76–77, 79–80, 143,
    167–168, 182
Judaism, 45
Judges, mentorship among, 182

K
Karate Kid series (films), 8, 69, 112
Kean University, 46
Kennedy, John F., 46
Kilpatrick, LaTonya, 110–117
The King of Staten Island (film), 56
Kiwanis, 34
Klein, Fred, 37–41, 81–82
Kobilka, Brian, 63

L
Larry Heiser Art Scholarship, xx
Lateral mentoring, 70–76
    at Colgate-Palmolive, 115
    at Deloitte, 120
    by Founding Fathers, 166
    by friends, 176
    in meetings, 80–82
    at The Mentor Project, xix, 149
    in the military, 128–129
    as new way to mentor, 163
    peer mentoring vs., 84–85
    in Silicon Valley, 172
    for start-up culture, 76–78
    and technology boom, 167–168
    trust in, 24–25
    on Wall Street, 133–134
    in the workplace, 78–80, 128–129
Law firms, 134–136
Lawrence Livermore National
        Laboratory, 101
Leaders, 113–114
Leading by example, 128
Lee, Bruce Y., 144
Lefkowitz, Robert, 59–64
Legacy:
    creating, with generativity, 13
    and generativity, 7
    as purpose of mentoring, 57–65
    and relationships, 90
Legacy trees, 59–65, 62f
Lepper, M. R., 21
Lerman, Zafra, 81
Lewis, Gabriel, xvii–xviii, 52
Life stages, 15f
LinkedIn, 34, 34–35, 158
Listservs, 183
Lobel, Debbie, 77, 78
Love and belongingness needs (Maslow's
        hierarchy of needs), 57
Lumeta, 50
Lunches, 182

M
McAdams, Dan, xii
McGrath, Quintin, 117–123
McGraw, Phil "Dr. Phil," 32
Madison, James, 166
Mahlon (biblical figure), 46
Markus, Hazel, 165
Marshall Bot, 160–161
Martin, Brian, 132–134, 136
Maslow, Abraham, 56–57

Massachusetts General Hospital (MGH), 83–84, 136
MasterMind groups, 34
Mattering, 48–49
Meaningful connections:
    at Colgate-Palmolive, 111, 113–116
    as component of mentoring, 23, 142
    creating, online, 159
    in different types of relationships, 30–31
    finding mentoring opportunities with, 186
    in the military, 130–131
    and workplace culture, 169
Meekin, Peter, 102
Meetings, 80–82
Mentees:
    benefits of mentoring for, 71
    coming full circle, 98–103
    finding, 180–181
    relationships between mentors and, 9–10, 88–89
Mentor (fictional character), 17, 45–46
Mentors, 87–108
    advisors vs., 28–31
    benefits of mentoring for, xiv–xvii, 71
    coaches vs., 41–43
    coming full circle, 98–103
    creating opportunities with or as, 181–182
    family friends as, 97–98
    finding, 179–180
    as focus of mentoring programs, 10–11, 122
    grandparents as, 94–96
    intrinsic motivation of, 9
    The Mentor Project, 103–108
    networking vs., 34–41
    professors as, 90–94
    relationships between mentees and, 9–10, 88–89
    sponsoring vs., 31–34
    teachers as, 87–90
Mentoring:
    accessibility of, xxi
    benefits of, to mentors, xiv–xvii
    in Bible, 46–48
    as component of generativity, xiii
    components of, 17–26, 70f
    defining, 146
    finding opportunities for, 179–187
    as form of generativity, 9–11
    future of, 157–164
    harnessing the power of, xx–xxi
    imperfect, 26
    as mandatory work practice, 112–113, 135–136

online, 159
    reasons for, 45–65
    roles similar to, 27–43
    by video, 161–164
Mentoring styles, 67–85
    hierarchical mentoring, 67–69, 71
    lateral mentoring, 70–76, 78–82
    peer mentoring, 82–85
    reverse mentoring, 69–70
    for start-up culture, 76–78
The Mentor Project:
    and Charlie Camarda, 76
    and Bill Cheswick, 51–52
    creating, xvii–xxi
    goal of, 147–148
    Innovation Lab at, 106
    lateral mentoring at, 77–78, 80–82
    as mentor-focused organization, 10
    and Lily Osman, 103–108
    sponsors helping form, 32–33
    video resources of, 161–162
    and Jura Zibas, 135
Mentorship culture, 165–177
    within communities, 171–173
    at Deloitte, 118
    within families, 173–174
    and Founding Fathers, 166–167
    within friendships, 174–177
    and technology boom, 167–168
    workplace culture as, 168–171
Meta (Facebook), 34, 35, 158, 172
MGH (Massachusetts General Hospital), 83–84, 136
Microsoft, 171
Military:
    lateral mentoring in, 128–129
    and safety, 129–132
    workplace mentoring in, 123–128
Misner, Charles, 91–94
Mondale, Walter, 149
Moriarty, Jim, xiv–xvi, 32
Morrow, Cynthia, 149, 153
Motivation:
    extrinsic motivation, 21–22, 30, 42
    intrinsic motivation, 9, 21–22, 57, 142
Mulally, Alan, 41
Mutual mentorship, 145

N
Naomi (biblical figure), 46–48
NASA, 20, 73–76
National Academies of Science, Engineering, and Medicine, 146

National Center for Education Statistics, 87
National Computer Security Center (NCSC), 100
National Institutes of Health (NIH), 60
National Security Agency (NSA), 100
Neimark, Jill, 6
Networking:
    mentoring vs., 34–41
    as possible benefit of mentoring, 113–114
Networking organizations, 183
NIH (National Institutes of Health), 60
Nobel Prize, 60–63
No Child Left Behind, 88
NSA (National Security Agency), 100

O
Obed (biblical figure), 47
Odysseus (fictional character), 17
Odyssey (Homer), 17, 45
Online networking, 34–35
Opportunities, for mentorship, 179–187
Oprah's Book Club, 32
Organized lunches, 182
Orman, Suze, 32
Orpah (biblical figure), 46
Osman, Lily, 103–107
Oz, Mehmet, 32

P
Pastan, Ira, 61
Peer mentoring, 82–85, 163
Personal computers, 168
Personal development, 112–117
Pfund, Christine, 146–147
PhD programs, 29
Philanthropy, xiii, 5
Physical development, 1, 2*f*
Physiological needs (Maslow's hierarchy of
    needs), 56
The Picture of Dorian Gray (Wilde), 13
Pine, 134
Post, Stephen, 6
Professional development, 112–117
Professors, as mentors, 90–94
Pugliese, Vincent (Vinny), 37–41

Q
Quayle, Dan, 149

R
Rabinovich, Avi, 81
Radner, Gilda, 54
Rebecca Bace Pioneer Award for Defensive
    Security, 103

Reciprocity:
    generativity vs., 6, 6*f*
    in mentoring, 4
    in mentoring relationship, 23
    in networking, 36
Recreation activities, 185
RedShred, 102
Relationships:
    building, 7–8
    leveraging, in crises, 129
    meaningful connections as, 12
    mentoring as, 26
    between mentors and mentees, 9–10, 88–89
    in networking, 34
Relevance, 4
Religion:
    as family culture, 174
    mentoring opportunities in, 184
Research, 141–155
    on aging, ix–xiv
    current state of, 153–155
    future directions for, 147–148
    goal of, 151–152
    learning objectives of, 152–153
    previous research, 145–147
    systemic reviews, 148–151
Retirement, 14
Retreats, 182
Revenge of the Nerds (film), 81
Reverse mentoring, 69–70
Rogers, Jenna, 146–147
Rotary Clubs, 34
Roth, Jesse, 61
Ruth (biblical figure), 46–48

S
Safety, 129–132
Safety needs (Maslow's hierarchy of needs), 57
Samms, Emma, 81
Samuelson, Peter, 81–82
Saturday Night Live, 54, 55
Scholarships for Women Studying Information
    Security (SWSIS), 103
Schwartzkopf, Norman, 81
Second-year projects, 29
Self-actualization needs (Maslow's hierarchy of
    needs), 57
Self-esteem, 57
"The Serendipitous Scientist" (Lefkowitz), 59–60
Silicon Valley, 171–173
Slack, 183
Snow, Jennifer, xviii, 32–33, 123–130
Social clubs, 184

Social media, 158–159, 183, 185
Spielberg, Steven, 81
Sponsorship, 31–34
Sports, 183, 184
Stagnation, 12–13
Stakeholder-Centered Coaching method, 41
Starbright Foundation, 81
Starbucks, 22
Starlight Children's Foundation, 81
Start-up culture, 76–78
Stone, Samantha, 149
Stoycheva, Valentina, 30
Strengths, focusing on others', 19
Students, advising, 28–29
Success, celebrating, 19–20
Suits (television program), 13
SWSIS (Scholarships for Women Studying
        Information Security), 103
Systemic reviews, 148–151

T
Taoism, 45
Tasks, in working alliances, 146
Teachers, as mentors, 87–90
Teams, mentoring, 119
Technology boom, 76, 167–168
Thompson, Justin, xx
Thompson, Lt. Colonel, 123–126, 128
TikTok, 161
Transactional, mentoring as, 9–10
Trust:
    as component of mentoring, 24–25, 142
    in friendships, 175
    in mentoring, 102, 126–128
    in the military, 130–131
Twitter (X), 158

U
The Unconscious (Weinberger and Stoycheva), 30
United Cerebal Palsy, 19
United States, founding of, 166–167
University of Maine, 91, 93
University of Maryland in College Park, 91
University of Wisconsin-Madison, 145
Usefulness, sense of, 4, 48–53

V
Validation, 4, 53–57
Van Groffrier, Graham, 93–94
Van Vliet, D., 49
Video, mentoring by, 161–164
Volunteering, xiii, 5
Vulnerability, 113, 135–136, 175

W
Wall Street, 132–134
Washington, George, 166
Watercoolers, 183
Weinberger, Aiden, 37
Weinberger, Joel, 28–30
Well-being, 56–57
What if the Moon Didn't Exist? (Comins), 91
WhatsApp, 183
Why Good Things Happen to Good People
        (Post and Neimark), 6
Wilde, Oscar, 13
Willy Wonka and the Chocolate Factory
        (film), 8
Wilson Elser, 134, 135
Winfrey, Oprah, 32
Wisdom, Jennifer, 149–153
Working alliances, 146–147
Workplaces:
    culture of, 168–171
    generativity in, 20–21
    hierarchical mentoring in, 68
    identity outside of, 14
    lateral mentoring in, 78–80
    leaving a legacy in, 58–59
    peer mentoring in, 83–85
Workplace mentoring, 109–139
    at Deloitte, 117–123
    in health care, 136–139
    lateral mentoring in, 128–129
    in law firms, 134–136
    in the military, 123–128
    personal and professional development
        enhanced by, 112–117
    and safety, 129–132
    on Wall Street, 132–134
Wozniak, Steve, 76–77, 79–80,
        167–168, 182

X
X (Twitter), 158
Xerox, 172

Y
Yachbes, Irene, xvii–xviii, 20–21, 23, 52
Yellow Berets, 60, 62*f*
YouTube, 161
Yun, Jeehye, 102–103

Z
Zibas, Jura, xvii–xviii, 52, 134–136
Zweibel, Alan, 54–57
Zweibel, Robin, 55